THE
MASTER KEY
TO POWER

The Condensed Classics Bundles Library

Infinite Mind Power
Leadership
Master Your Mind!
Money Magic!
Napoleon Hill's Golden Classics
Success Dynamite
Success Secrets of the Great Masters
The Power of Optimism

THE MASTER KEY TO POWER

The Power of Faith
by Norman Vincent Peale

The Power of Awareness
by Neville Goddard

The Power of Concentration
by Theron Q. Dumont

Power and Wealth
by Ralph Waldo Emerson

Atom-Smashing Power of Mind
by Charles Fillmore

abridged and introduced by
Mitch Horowitz

Published 2020 by Gildan Media LLC
aka G&D Media.
www.GandDmedia.com

The Power of Faith was originally published as *Faith Is the Answer* by Smiley Blanton, M.D. and Norman Vincent Peale, D.D. in 1940.
The Power of Awareness was originally published in 1952.
The Power of Concentration was originally published in 1916.
Power and *Wealth* were first published in Ralph Waldo Emerson's collection *The Conduct of Life* in 1860.
Atom-Smashing Power of Mind was originally published in 1949.
The Power of Awareness was originally published in 1952.
Abridgement and Introduction copyright © 2020 by Mitch Horowitz

No part of this book may be reproduced or transmitted in any form, by any means, (electronic, photocopying, recording, or otherwise) without the prior written permission of the author. No liability is assumed with respect to the use of the information contained within. Although every precaution has been taken, the author and publisher assume no liability for errors or omissions. Neither is any liability assumed for damages resulting from the use of the information contained herein.

Cover design by David Rheinhardt of Pyrographx

Interior design by Meghan Day Healey of Story Horse, LLC.

ISBN: 978-1-7225-0330-7

Contents

Introduction
7

The Power of Faith
by Norman Vincent Peale
9

The Power of Awareness
by Neville Goddard
73

The Power of Concentration
by Theron Q. Dumont
111

Power and Wealth
by Ralph Waldo Emerson
191

Atom-Smashing Power of Mind
by Charles Fillmore
239

About Mitch Horowitz
295

Introduction

In the Name of Power

Have you ever noticed how little we as a culture talk frankly about *power*?

For all our reticence to mention it, the search for power animates individuals, corporations, religions, and nations. Yet the term power is rarely used, as though to even acknowledge it is to admit to corruption.

The abridged works in this collection make a blunt and refreshing admission of the desirability of power. Speaking personally, I grew far more relaxed and satisfied with my search and strivings in the world when I came to acknowledge to myself and to others that I sought power. Power quite simply means possessing the personal agency to achieve your aims in life.

But—and this point is vital—true power must be pursued with ethics. It must be generative. The only way to renew power is through equitable exchange of goods, services, and ideas. Otherwise what results is not power at all. It is brutality, either on a personal or macro scale.

I believe that the five works in this collection, each of which features its own individual introduction by me, will unlock for you the means to amass power that is wed to ethics, productivity, and personal nobility. This is the kind of power that you can be unashamed to pursue—and to wield.

—Mitch Horowitz

The Power of Faith

The Power of Faith

*The Founding Father
of Positive Thinking On
How to Lead a Healthful Life*

Norman Vincent Peale

THE CONDENSED CLASSICS LIBRARY™

Contents

INTRODUCTION
The Foundations of Positive Thinking 15

CHAPTER ONE
The Power of Faith 18

CHAPTER TWO
The Hidden Energies of the Mind 26

CHAPTER THREE
Fear, Worry, and Anxiety 37

CHAPTER FOUR
Conscience and the Sense of Guilt 46

CHAPTER FIVE
Self-Criticism, Failure, and Success 51

CHAPTER SIX
Grief and Sorrow 55

CHAPTER SEVEN
The Company of the Lonely 60

CHAPTER EIGHT
Love and Marriage 65

CHAPTER NINE
The Faith That Heals 68

ABOUT THE AUTHOR 71

Introduction

The Foundations of Positive Thinking

by Mitch Horowitz

This short book is a condensation of Norman Vincent Peale's first collaboration with psychiatrist Smiley Blanton, originally titled *Faith Is the Answer*. Their 1940 effort presents a valuable summary of Peale's therapeutic theology and of the themes he explored to worldwide notice twelve years later in his *Power of Positive Thinking*.

But in *The Power of Faith* you will discover a different Norman Vincent Peale from the one who later authored one of the world's most popular books.

The authorial voice of *The Power of Faith* reveals the younger Peale not only as a trenchant and elegant writer, but also as a figure of considerable literary breadth. In *The Power of Faith*, Peale effortlessly weaves Scriptural analysis and little-known works of theology with the ethical insights of figures including Marcus Aurelius, William James, Henry Drummond, and Daniel Defoe, as well as the modern voices of his own congregants.

Peale wanted to be understood not only as a theologian of good tidings, but also as a true intellectual, which he was. One of the pains of Peale's life was that, despite his worldwide fame and in some ways because of it, he got rundown in lettered circles after the publication of *The Power of Positive Thinking*. Critics and academics, many of whom I doubt read or more than skimmed Peale's books, often depicted the minister a kind of philosopher for simpletons. This was a profoundly unfair judgment, which I explore in my historical treatment of Peale in *One Simple Idea: How Positive Thinking Reshaped Modern Life*.

The Power of Faith is less mystical in nature than many of Peale's later works. The minister had not yet fully immersed himself in the study of New Thought, Science of Mind, Christian Science, and other variants of the mind metaphysics that characterized *The Power of Positive Thinking*. Yet the telltale influence of early twentieth-century French mind theorist Emile Coué appears in *The Power of Faith*. In Peale's chapter on self-criticism he notes, "imagination is stronger than will." That was one of Coué's key insights. Coué noted that our behavioral patterns are dictated by subliminal emotion and self-image much more than by personal determination. Hence, Coué—who coined the mantra "day by day, in every way, I am getting better and better"—considered self-reconditioning essential to the pursuit of a happy and purposeful life. Peale's resonance with this principle warmed him to concepts he later discovered in New Thought, including the therapeutic uses of visualization, prayer, and affirmation. You will see that Peale also examines the Proverb "as a man thinketh," which served as the basis of the spiritual-psychology brought by early New Thought author James Allen in 1903.

Peale and psychiatrist Smiley Blanton originally wrote this book in alternating chapters. My condensation retains only the key points of Peale's own chapters. In some cases, Blanton's considerable psychological insights have been supplanted by more recent developments in neuroscience, cognitive restructuring, and psychopharmacology. But Peale's spiritual observations and Scriptural analyses remain universal, actionable, and revealing of his earliest attitudes toward the therapeutic value of faith.

I believe that in this book you will discover Norman Vincent Peale not only as a deeply appealing storyteller and communicator, but also as a man whose vision of religion as a workable, practical philosophy helped transform the spiritual landscape of the past century—and of our own. His early vision may transform your life, as well.

Chapter One

The Power of Faith

If I were to tell you that everything troubling you, every weakness, every unhappiness can be eliminated; if I were to declare that everything about your life can be strong and effective, what would be your reaction? Probably many of you would be skeptical or at least wistful, doubtful that such marvelous results are possible. Some people have never had anything great happen to them, so they doubt that it can happen. They suffer from what a great thinker once referred to as "the vast inertia of the soul."

But it is a fact that any person's life can be so completely changed that every crippling thing known and unconscious which interferes with his well-being can be eliminated or effectively controlled. This is no academic assertion but one that can be fully documented from the experiences of many people in whom the most amazing results were obtained. These people learned the technique of faith and so tapped a curative element so potent that no malady of personality could resist its health-giving force. And like many epoch-making processes, it operates simply.

You may develop the art of having faith through two suggestions, if they are faithfully followed: (1) the practice of simple but habitual prayer and devotional meditation;

(2) the surrender of your life in childlike trust to the will of God.

We shall now proceed to explain the content and operation of this workable formula.

The late Henry Drummond was one of the superior intellects and scholars of his time. Beyond this, he was a spiritual genius, one of those rare characters who gain acute insight into spiritual laws. Drummond's secret was so simple that anyone can put it into practice. He stated his formula as follows: "Ten minutes spent in Christ's society every day, aye, two minutes, will make the whole day different." Multiply one day by every day and add the cumulative effect of habit and the changed mental outlook, and you will understand how this brief period faithfully observed can change everything, even to your entire life.

We have all known men who have been like saints—strong, radiantly happy. Examination of their daily program reveals regular periods of spiritual meditation. Drummond tells us that a few minutes daily spent in thinking about Christ and in consciously and sincerely seeking to secure his power will make the whole day different. This simple practice gives control over fears, weaknesses, and those tragic ineptitudes which interfere so disastrously with success in life.

Wordsworth was another who discovered the amazing values in a daily period of spiritual meditation. Wordsworth's method was unusual but exceedingly rewarding if we may judge by the quality of his mind and character.

It was his custom every day to meditate on a few of Jesus' words, reading them slowly and endeavoring to bring out their full meaning. He would stop and say, "I wonder what Jesus meant when he said that. What was the expression on his face, the tone of his voice?" This approach served to make Christ come near to Wordsworth as a vital living character and to walk with him in his own time.

The hurry and rush of our lives is often advanced as a reason why the daily period of personal prayer and meditation is impossible today. This, of course, is a specious excuse, for we have ample time for what we want to do. It is possible for every person to go apart alone for at least ten minutes every day to relax body, mind, and soul, open himself to God and allow the divine energies to flood his receptive spirit.

There is a quality of the mind through which, with practice, we can retire into ourselves, open a little door, and be in our own quiet inner temple. On a train, or bus, or rushing subway we may close our eyes, turn our minds to Christ and withdraw from the busy world into a few minutes of communion that will give us calm strength and imperturbable poise for the day.

I stress this practice, for it is a certain and workable method for developing faith. The result of this habitual daily meditation is that we come finally to believe absolutely in him and consequently develop a depth of faith that is sure and positive. Live with Christ in daily spiritual associations and your faith in God will be deep and certain.

This makes God a real factor rather than a vague concept. An old blind Indian in the West, a magnificent person with inner peace and kindly spirit, revealed the source of his strength when he said, "it is easy to believe in God when you live alone with him in the dark." He knew how to have faith because spiritually he lived with God.

I could write page after page of theory about how to have faith, but I will save you much reading, and myself much labor of writing, by saying that if you will definitely set aside a few minutes, ten or even five, or, as Drummond says, two minutes, to think about God and Christ, to confess your sins, to pray for those who have done wrong against you, and to ask for strength, and if you do this consistently day after day, a true faith will before long begin to send spiritual health and power through your personality.

A Chinese gentleman, a successful broker, recently told his story in our Church Clinic. It was a spiritual narrative, full of tragedy and rising to stirring drama. He came of a wealthy family and had every opportunity that wealth and social connections afford. He ultimately lost his wife through his dissipation and his money went the same way, the bulk of it through gambling. His health failed and a nervous breakdown made him unfit for any except very limited activity. At this juncture he met some people whose joy and delight in life amazed him. It awakened the hope that there might be a way out of his sad failure. They told him the way was by faith, but the advice was futile. Faith was just the thing he did not have either in God, his fellow man, or himself. But he was one of those rare souls who, once being convinced of great possibilities, is not daunted by any obstacle however formidable.

He began a daily plan of communion with God, that being on the advice of a wise friend the sure method of gaining faith. Perseverance was difficult because of his nervous state and the dulled condition of his mind. But he kept at it desperately, feeling it was his last hope. For thirty minutes each morning he gave himself to a period of meditation and asked four questions:

What have I to thank God for during the last twenty-four hours?

What sins have I committed in the last twenty-four hours?

What does God want me to do?

Whom should I pray for?

The first two questions he limited to twenty-four hours because the memory is inclined not to be specific unless the period of analysis is short.

Our Chinese friend's story ended with his finding a restored life. He overcame his disability, his mind began to function with its old time efficiency. He is today a happy man.

Sometimes in my interviews, when deep springs of experience have been opened, I have clearly felt the presence of Christ. It was so when this gentleman asserted his positive conviction that faith in God has remade his entire life, even to his health and business acumen.

And now the second and ultimate method for having faith is simply to have faith. Many people get lost exploring abstruse procedures, unaware that the secret is to believe by an act of trust. It was for this reason that Christ, the supreme Teacher, told us we could not enter his kingdom until we had a childlike heart.

The New Testament says, "According to your faith be it unto you." We receive good in direct proportion to the amount of faith we exercise. "Lord, I believe; help thou my unbelief," is the attitude that opens the door to new life. In plain vernacular that means, "I trust you, O Lord. I believe, even though I cannot see how it can be. I believe even though shadowy questions haunt my mind." The spirit struggles to believe, triumphing over the weak doubtings of the earth-bound body. The release of power that comes with this victory of faith is the most impressive phenomenon of human experience.

I was asked to call on a patient in a tuberculosis hospital. This man said he had been helped by my radio program and wanted to talk with me. I went to see him at considerable expenditure of time, for the hospital was some distance from the city, but it proved to be very worthwhile—one of my most inspiring and enlightening experiences. I found this man lying on a mattress on a board because of the condition of his spine. His hand was off at the wrist, but he was one of the happiest men I ever met all my life long. I who had gone to comfort him was myself comforted, even thrilled by the story he told.

He was taken to the hospital in 1936 and given up to die. He had been a successful lawyer, with a wife and two sons. Everything he owned went into the battle to save his life.

At the time he became hospitalized he was having frequent hemorrhages with severe pain. He was in an apparently hopeless condition. It was at this juncture that he listened to the radio talk in which occurred this quotation from the New Testament, "I can do all things through Christ which strengthens me."

"You said," he explained, "whoever you are, wherever you are, and in whatever condition or circumstance, if you surrender your life completely to God and put your trust in him, you can obtain Divine power by which you can win over anything."

"You also spoke of the amount of faith that would help us. 'Even as a grain of mustard seed.' This seemed to me like a small investment for the return offered."

Looking straight at me, this man said, "I had heard that sort of thing all my life—that is, when I went to church, which was not too often—and it never moved me. In fact," he continued, "I guess I never really knew what it meant. I'm sure I didn't appreciate how deep it went. But this time," he declared, "it came over me as by a wave that it was true. I bowed my head," he went on, "and did just as you said. I guess I was at the end of my rope and I meant it absolutely when I put my life in God's hands. A strange thing happened. I felt a surge of peace. I came to have a conviction that regardless of the number and pain of hemorrhages nothing could ever hurt me again. I went farther, repeating my surrender every day, several times a day, and one day I came to believe that my hemorrhages would stop. That was late in 1936, and in early 1937 they did stop and I've had none to this day." (This conversation took place in 1939.)

With a happy smile, the narrator continued: "I am slowly getting better, but that is not the chief thing that has happened to me. The main thing is the strange new strength, this wonderful inner peace, this absolute sense of being attached to the very power of God himself. We, my family and I, have had to face many difficult problems. Again and again we have been caught in what seemed a blind alley with no way out, but God opened a way every time, and he always will."

I sat there looking at that heroic and inspiring man. I was listening to one of the most amazing accounts of God's grace that has ever come to my attention. We both knew that day that we were talking about no imaginary happening but were awed by the real experience of a man who in his dire need stumbled upon the greatest thing that can happen to a human being—the actual release, through faith, of the power of God into human experience. There is in religious faith and for our benefit a greater power than we realize.

Chapter Two

The Hidden Energies of the Mind

"Men habitually use only a small part of the powers which they possess and which they might use under appropriate circumstances." The eminent psychologist William James, great genus in understanding personality, said this. Every person has it in him to be far more and accomplish far more, according to this great expert in personality.

Deep within every normal individual is a vast reservoir of untapped power waiting to be used. In most of us only a small trickle of power is seeping to the surface, and on that we live and do our work. It is little wonder that many of us are tired and unhappy, frustrated and ineffectual. A sixteen-cylinder car, if it possessed feeling and reason, would not be very happy, or in any sense satisfactory, if it went sputtering and limping along on one cylinder. That is exactly what most of us are doing. This book is intended to help people learn and practice the secret of using all their power and ability.

The first step toward being what you can be is to know what you are. That is to say, no man can have the use of all his potential power until he learns to understand himself. The trouble with so many people who fail in this life is that they go through the world thinking deep within them that they are ordinary, commonplace persons. Thus, having no fundamental belief in themselves, they dissipate their energies in undisciplined living. Such persons live aimless and erratic lives very largely because they never had a glimpse of what life really can be and what they can become. There exist possibilities for successful living in the unconscious mind. How can they be released and how can religion help?

A man has a good book in his hand when he turns the pages of the Bible. Why does the Bible retain its hold on humanity after hundreds of years? The answer, of course, is that the Bible contains more than any book ever written, the most astute insight into, and knowledge of, human beings.

In it is a story of a young man who became fed up on the orderly, decent life at the old home, and, getting a sizable sum of money from his father, went off and drank it up. We are told he went into "a far country," which is indeed an apt description. It is a far country, for some get so far into it they never get back. But this boy did get back. When his money was gone, his job lost, and he had gone the rounds of his associates getting only the cold shoulder, "He came to himself," as the Bible says with eloquent finality.

Here is an example of the remarkable insight of the Bible. Here is a man, ruining himself not because he was wicked, but because he was ignorant about himself. When he came to himself, when he came to his senses, he had the inestimable thrill of self-discovery. He saw, as in a flash, that he was on the wrong track; that he was really throwing his energies, his abilities, and his future away. "He came to himself" and saw with sharp discernment what he was and what he could become. Then, continues the Bible, he said, "I will arise." From then on life is an onward, upward movement. It becomes aggressive, victorious living.

Christianity is coming to be more widely recognized every day as possessing the surest techniques for helping people realize themselves. It has an astounding genius for touching men's ordinary lives and unlocking doors behind which their personalities have long atrophied. Many people have the mistaken notion that religion restricts and imprisons. On the contrary, sin does that, while religion swings open the door and invites men out to freer and happier lives. An old hymn sings of Christ, "He sets the prison free," and that, of course, is what many ineffectual people are—prisoners. They are prisoners of the senses, prisoners of social customs, prisoners of themselves. Christ sets them free, when, coming to themselves, they say, "I will arise and go to my Father."

One element in the adventure of self-discovery is to become aware of our innate goodness. Whether you are prepared to admit it or not, you *are* a good person basically. No man can go far in unworthy living without provoking the increasing protests of the finer self. It is impossible for any man long to escape the relentless challenge of the great personality in his soul.

Some years ago a distinguished playwright wrote a play that bore the title, *Six Characters in Search of an Author.*

This was Luigi Pirandello. The play pictured a rehearsal at which several characters came bursting in, demanding to be played by the actors. That is an accurate picture of our lives. On our life's stage great characters burst out from within us demanding to identify themselves with us, to perform in us before the world.

Nathanial Hawthorne left among his papers an outline of a play, which he never wrote, but which intrigues us with its possibilities. It was to be a play in which the principal character never appears. Hawthorne with his superb genius could have made much of such an idea, but he did not have to write it for us, for you and I have lived it often enough. It is tragic to think of a man playing on the stage of life only the minor, and often unworthy, parts that are in him. He is the bigot, the coward, the defeated spirit, the sinner, the liar, or the cheat. But for a man never to play the principal character within himself—that is tragical. Never to perceive and act the hero in his life; never to see the Galahad within him, never to see the saint in him—that is deepest tragedy; that is indeed to have the principal character never appear.

In every weak person there is a strong person. In every evil person is a good person. In every defeated person is a victorious person. To become aware of this nobility and power within ourselves, is to know and to be able to practice the Art of Living.

This adventure of self-discovery is working out along another great line. Many people are discovering through their religious faith that in themselves there is a great old rugged character whom no one can discourage or defeat. Many modern people whom I happen to know had received so many blows and hard knocks that the come-back spirit, had all but gone from them. They were about ready to admit they were defeated and that they could do nothing about it except complain and grow bitter.

I have seen scores, even hundreds, of men and women turn to religious faith in earnest attempt to get power into their lives. I have seen them come, saying, "Lord, I am run down, my life is empty, circumstances are too strong for me—I can no longer do anything by my own strength." Then I have seen them do the wisest thing in the world, which is to turn the switch and contact the circuit of creative spiritual energy; that is, to put their lives, with all problems, completely into God's hands. This they have done, with wholehearted faith that God is interested in them and will turn his power into their lives like water into a reservoir long empty and dry. In the Bible we read, "But as many as received him, to them gave he power," and so He does, and modern people are finding out this great secret in increasing numbers every day.

A young businessman in his late thirties told me his experience. He was brought up in a devout home, but like many others, drifted away from the religious life in college days. Later he married and got into business and social life, and the church would see him at Easter, but that was about all. His connection with spiritual values was exceedingly tenuous. Then hard times came. Business grew difficult. His domestic situation became complicated. His and his wife's life were rooted only in material things, and such roots are insecure. To sum it up, his life crashed in on him and his courage ran out. Life had rained blow after blow upon him, and it was almost more than the spirit could bear.

Then he encountered a radiant personality who seemed to possess a depth of peace and confidence in a situation not unlike his own, a man who was not beaten. On the contrary, he was overcoming adversity by an unwavering perseverance and sustained attack. My friend saw that this man was being fed by what seemed an unfailing stream of power. He asked the secret and the answer was, Christ.

"Why, I have always believed in Christ," my friend said.

"Yes," the other man replied, "but have you ever absolutely and completely given yourself into his hands?"

My friend was forced to admit that he hadn't, but that state didn't last long. He turned to Christ in faith. Live wires now tap his personality and a spiritual transformer has stepped up his physical and mental energy. He said an interesting thing to me recently.

"All my life," he declared, "I have been more or less around religion, but it always seemed a rather dead thing to me. Strange, how different it is now." And then he concluded, "But one thing is sure, when you actually take it into your life spiritually, it does everything it says it will."

Layer upon layer of childhood influences form in the unconscious mind the basis of our moral nature. Religion attempts to govern the fundamental instincts and impulses by saturating the mind with spiritual ideals to such an extent that the automatic functioning of a man's life will be on a basis of strength and goodness. Religion teaches us to allow only good and beautiful thoughts to enter the unconscious because of the obvious fact often demonstrated that the unconscious can only send back what was first sent down. Let in bad thoughts freely and bad motivation will be sent back. Habitually send in thoughts of an elevated nature and the unconscious will inevitably return attitudes and actions of a corresponding quality.

As William James pointed out, the molecules and cells of our bodies and brains are storing up day by day every action, emotion, and thought to use either for or against us, quite automatically, in crises which ultimately arrive.

The Bible expresses the deepest insight into human nature in a well-known phrase, "As he thinketh in his heart, so is he." That is one of the profoundest truths ever set down for man's guidance. The word "heart" is used to describe the inmost part of man's thought and feeling; in all likelihood what the modern psychiatrist refers to as "the unconscious." That is to say, a man is in the last analysis what he has been predominantly sending into the controlling center of his life.

The ideas or thoughts which finally determine our actions and character are not those which we receive and examine in the conscious mind. It is not "as a man thinketh in his conscious mind" that constitutes his personality. That is only a receiving station, or perhaps it can be compared to a reception office, where thoughts, good, bad, and innocuous, are examined and passed upon. Some are rejected. If these rejected thoughts are evil, their temporary presence in the conscious mind has done little if any harm. If they are good thoughts, they have had little opportunity to have any effect. But the thought, good or bad, which is received hospitably and is ushered into the mind repeatedly with a welcome, becomes eventually the thought a man "thinketh in his heart," and presently it may be said, "So is he."

People come to us complaining of having what they describe as "bad thoughts." These are thoughts of hate, or immorality, or dishonesty, or sometimes even murder. These people are troubled by the feeling that the thought which passed through the mind has made them guilty of sin. Sometimes they have quoted the Biblical passage, "Whosoever looketh on a woman to lust after her, hath committed adultery with her already in his heart."

No sin is committed if a thought enters the mind, provided it is not made welcome. The thought first passes into an anteroom, where it stands before the mind acting as a judge. No matter how sordid or evil, it has not touched the personality with its infamy or in any way laid guilt upon the soul unless and until the mind acting as judge admits it with a welcome. If the mind decides against it and dismisses it, the personality is not only unsullied, but is, on the contrary, by this act of rejection stimulated and strengthened in moral power. You cannot prevent the birds from flying over your head but you can keep them from building nests in your hair.

A thought that enters the mind, is weighed and rejected, and is passed, condemned, from the mind, leaves no stain of guilt but instead greatly increases spiritual power.

There can be no doubt that Jesus held this point of view, for in the passage quoted above the phrase, "Looketh on a woman to lust after her" does not imply a passing and unadmitted impure thought but a definitely entertained desire. The word "lust," which is the important word in the passage, means a premeditated and active attitude implying an idea welcomed and pleasurably entertained.

In my experience as pastor I have known many people whose lives were made exceedingly unhappy by their failure to make this wholehearted distinction between the evil thought examined and rejected and an evil thought accepted and entertained.

Consideration of this problem, which affects so many people, makes it plain that a conscious mind, clear, penetrating, morally discriminating and vigorous, standing guard over the unconscious mind, is profoundly essential equipment for happy and effective living.

That which is received and accepted by the conscious mind determines ultimately the automatic reaction of the unconscious and in effect may be summed up as character. Before every deed there is a thought or more properly a succession of thoughts. Before the thief steals with his hand he steals with his mind. Before the immoral act is preformed the mind has already committed the offense. If the thought of a wrong act has never been favorably entertained by the mind, the act itself will never take place. The issue is determined, not at the moment of crisis by rational and objective thinking, but by the resistance or lack of it in the unconscious, a resistance which has been strengthened or weakened each time the conscious mind rejected or accepted the thought.

In a certain small town one family had operated the local bank for three generations. Grandfather, father, and son in succession had filled the important position of banker to the community. The family was held in the highest esteem and respect. The Great Depression came, and the son, who had become president of the bank, had been lured by the speculation mania sweeping the country and had overtaxed his ability to meet his obligations. He had to have money.

One night, alone in the bank, the thought of falsifying the books came to him, but he resolutely put it aside. It returned again and again. No one would ever know. He could make good out of his earnings before the bank examiners would discover the default. The pressure became great. In other relationships, as it later appeared, he had played fast and loose with fidelity. His inner supports had been weakened.

The unconscious could only return what he had given it, and one night the hand crept out hesitantly but surely to perform the deed which sent him to the penitentiary and broke the long and honored tradition of a fine family. "As he thinketh in his heart, so is he." What we are will eventually appear. The mask will some day slip from the face. The truth will out.

In the unconscious are all the forces which make for our success or failure, our misery or our happiness. These forces according to their strength control the mind, determining our choices and decisions. In the unconscious lie hidden energies which can defeat us if not understood and properly used but which wisely used can endow us with great power. Religion says that when these hidden energies are brought under the influence of Christ as Master of life, the most amazing results appear in people whose lives were hitherto commonplace or defeated.

By the phrase "coming under the influence of Christ" we mean the acceptance of Christ's way of life as our own. Further than that, it requires an attitude which we like to call spiritual experience. The standard word for it is "conversion." It is a surrender of self to God by an act of faith, a wholehearted readiness to follow God's will.

This spiritual experience goes deeply into the personality laying a controlling hand upon the unconscious mind, the inner life force, holding firmly in check the destructive elements and releasing the hidden energies to produce a person of wisdom and power.

CHAPTER THREE

Fear, Worry, and Anxiety

There are many businessmen in America today who are failing in business or not getting ahead. The free functioning of their intellectual and emotional capacities is inhibited by anxiety and fear. Here, for example, is a man who goes down to his office in the morning and sits down to a desk full of business.

This man needs to be able to draw upon every bit of his mental equipment in order to dispose effectively of the problems before him. But he is haunted by anxiety and fear. He is worried about the condition of the stock market, about meeting the payroll, or about holding his job. He worries about the war in Europe or the condition of this country. He worries about his family, or how to meet the payments on his home. He worries about whether he has heart trouble or high blood pressure, or fears that some sin he committed will catch up with him and put its bony and terrifying finger into his business to his undoing. His powers should be drawn to a focus as the divergent rays of the sun are caught by the glass and brought to a point of heat. But his powers are drawn off in a score of different directions by the wide sprouting of his anxieties, and the emotional and mental energy which he needs for success is lacking. Deeply buried anxiety in the unconscious mind is the cause of an astoundingly large number of inefficient and desultory careers in our time.

"What is courage?" a small boy recently asked his mother, and then added, "Is it like our cat when he arches his back and spits when he is afraid?"

His mother tried to think of a way to make the real meaning of courage clear to her son, for she believed that the first and finest lesson that parents can teach little children is courage. She took him for a long walk in the country, and they finally came to a place where a destructive forest fire had raged. In a blackened, fire-swept field they saw one little red flower.

Pointing to that little, courageous, optimistic red flower, she said, "There is courage, my son—a fragile red flower growing in a fire-swept land." It is a good symbol of courage. Soon or late, the fires of adversity will roar across the life of each one of us, and in the blackened desolation that remains it will be hard to see any hope, but in that hour we must project the flower of courage in a fire-swept land. That one flower of courage will be the forerunner of restored life.

What is the cure for anxiety and fear? How many have this kind of courage? The best answer to that question is not any comment of mine or suggestion from the experts but is a statement found in the Bible which reads, "Take no thought for your life, what ye shall eat, or what ye shall drink; nor yet for your body, what ye shall put on . . . But seek ye first the kingdom of God and his righteousness; and all these things shall be added unto you."

What does that mean? It means that we are not to worry about the necessities of life, but to strive for inner peace and mental, emotional, and spiritual harmony, developing an organized and integrated personality which will be able to meet life so effectively that these necessary things will indeed "be added unto you." This admonition from the Bible implies what is directly stated in many other Scripture references—that an habitual resting of our worries upon the goodness of God through real faith releases a power into our lives which is not of this world, the power of God, through which we accomplish what otherwise would be impossible.

One of the practical ways of putting into practice this wise advice is to develop the habit of not talking about our anxieties and our worries. The average anxious person is constantly telling everybody how worried and apprehensive he is about everything. It should be recalled that speech has greater effect on emotion than thinking has. An actor, for example, can talk himself into the desired emotions he wishes to portray. Get your anxiety out of your general conversations and it will tend to drop out of your mind. On the other hand, it is advisable to go to someone who has the insight and skill to help you become free from your worries.

Go to your minister, or your priest, or your rabbi, or to your psychiatrist and unburden yourself. Tell everything that is on your heart, including your sins, real and imaginary, the haunting sense of guilt, and every suppressed desire. This confession, this unburdening of yourself will throw sunlight into every dark corner of the mind, drive out the shadows, bring blessed relief, and open the way for complete healing of the malady of anxiety.

Religion is a practical method for solving this problem. Many people do not understand present-day religious practice; they think of it as something dull and musty, quite remote from real life. Thereby they miss the one thing that could make them happy and successful and useful. Some time ago I was in the police station—a voluntary visit—and in talking with the burly sergeant I told him I had just given a radio talk on "How Religion Can Conquer Nervousness." He was astounded and said: "I never heard of religion having anything to do with nervousness. I thought religion was just going to church and acting as decent as you can."

"Go read your Bible," I replied, "and you will find religion is a medicine for every human ill."

"I sure will," he said, "because if religion can do what you say, I'll have to try a little."

It will do everything it claims to do for the man who really tries it.

How does the fact that we turn to God in trust and faith relieve us of our fears? For one thing, when a man gets his mind on God, he gets it off himself. Fears, in reality, accompany excessive thinking about oneself. They are nurtured by the ego-centered attitude as a nest is warmed by a sitting hen. Our minds sit on the nest of our real and imaginary fears, and they grow up rapidly. We need to engage in more physical activity and less introspection if we are to eliminate fear from our lives.

Mary Ellen Chase writes in *The Good Fellowship*: "Manual labor to my father was not only good and decent for its own sake, but, as he was given to saying, it straightened out one's thoughts—a contention which I have since proved on many occasions; indeed, the best antidote I know to a confused head or to tangled emotions is to work with one's hands. To scrub a floor has alleviated many a broken heart, and to wash and iron one's clothes has brought order and clarity to many a perplexed and anxious mind."

For this reason a well-known psychologist very wisely advised a young man to run around the block every night until he was dead tired, as an effective means toward conquering his fears.

But there are other and better things to do to conquer fear than run around the block. The one sure method of eradicating fear from the mind is by surrendering one's life to God. By that I mean avoiding the mistake of attempting to pluck fear out by a process of effort and struggle or by power of will. This only serves to implant it more firmly in the consciousness. The surrender of life to God means that all fear and worry is laid before Him and the future is left in His hands in perfect trust. We are then able to avoid any worried thought for the morrow, for God knows our needs and will take care of us.

For my part, I have found it absolutely true that when I sincerely put my life in God's hands and trust him to take care of me, he does so with amazing fidelity and kindliness. This is one of the greatest secrets in the world. It gives any man peace and strength beyond calculation. Let all your fears go—give them to God. He will not let you down. Did you ever carry a tired child in your arms? You will recall the complete relaxation of the little body. The child rests in your arms perfectly free from tension. There is in him no fear that he will be dropped. Feeling this trust, you hold the little form all the closer and with the greater care, for you cannot fail such complete confidence.

If this kind of love and faith passes between grown-ups and tired, sleepy children, how much more profoundly does God take to his heart adults who are tired and worn in the dark nights of this life?

A stout heart and a courageous spirit constitute a basic necessity for this life. Samuel Johnson understood this fact when he said that courage is the primary virtue! "Unless a man have that virtue, he has no security for preserving any other."

I once spoke to the students of a New England university, and afterward went home to dinner with an old and very wise professor. As we sat by the fire that stormy day, he presented me with a little book by J.M. Barrie, saying, "You will need this often. Make a companion of it."

He was right. It was Barrie's famous essay on "Courage," and I have always kept it nearby. Its deep philosophy, written in his inimitable style, has meant much when my courage has ebbed. In it, among other things, Barrie says: "Pray for courage with your daily bread, for courage will keep you lighthearted and gay and you must keep lighthearted and gay."

How to have courage is a practical problem faced by every reader of this volume.

In a terrifying scene, Lady Macbeth—strong, masterful as well as cruel—strove to buttress her husband's ebbing courage. "But if we fail?" he asked, timorously. "Screw your courage to the sticking-place," she belligerently declared, "and we'll not fail." Granted that this illustration comes through the commission of a famous crime, it nevertheless portrays an important fact about life. There come times when courage ebbs and some more vigorous personality may admonish us to screw our courage to the sticking place. That is exactly what we must do—but how to do it?

One of the most pathetic things in the world is to see human beings struggling against great odds, trying desperately to screw their courage to the sticking place. It is pathetic, but it is also inspiring, for it reveals the magnificent heroism of the average man. The more we watch people fighting gallantly against discouragement and hardship and pain and fear, the more wonderful we feel they are. The great need of this life is to develop courage.

Many people miss the best rewards of life simply because of their inability to screw their courage to the sticking place and keep it there until the game is won. Browsing through an old library recently, I came across a book written by a very wise man of a bygone generation. The book told a story showing that ebbing courage has been a problem in every generation.

Its author had a friend who had acquired a claim in a far Western gold field. The claim was in a lonely spot in the mountains. When the friend started to dig for gold, he found evidence that much work had been done on the claim a long while before. Farthest in, in the excavation he found an old rusted pick, its handle rotted off but its point sticking firmly in the rocky soil. He threw the pick aside and went to work and to his amazement, just a few feet beyond where he had found it, he came upon a rich vein of gold. He could not escape thinking about the tragedy of the old pick, and sometime later he heard the story.

A prospector had learned of the probability of a rich strike in this locality, had staked out his claim and had gone to work. Day after day, until his back ached unbearably, he worked with his pick, but never a glimpse of gold did he see. Gradually, the acid of discouragement crept through his system, eating away his resolution. His courage slowly ebbed, and one day in desperation, and with a sense of complete futility, he drove his pick hard into the rocky earth, gathered up his belongings, and went away. The passing years rusted the pick and ate away the handle.

The tragedy of ebbing courage which failed just short of success, was not revealed until the prospector of our story many years later came and found, a few feet farther on, the vein which would have fallen to the first man had he been able to solve the problem of failing courage. The man is fortunate indeed who, no matter how desperate his condition, how unpromising his prospects, still has growing within his soul the red flower of courage.

What is the secret of this kind of courage? When courage fails the secret is to fill your mind and saturate your consciousness with simple and trusting faith in God. I emphasize this procedure, for it is the heart of the problem of fear.

There is a quotation from the Bible which every man with ebbing courage would do well to hang on his bedroom wall, where he could look at it every morning before starting out to face the day's struggle and every evening so that it might leaven his unconscious mind as he slept. That great sentence is this, "In all these things we are more than conquerors through him that loved us."

Now, I do not mean to say that every person who belongs to the church, or who believes academically in God, has the kind of faith that keeps courage from ebbing. But I do say that every individual I have ever known who truly practices the faith of the New Testament always kept a sturdy heart. I have never yet known a man who believes in and practices—and the emphasis is on "practices"—sincere faith in God to be defeated. I can produce scores of present-day people, young and old, from every walk of life who will tell you from their own experience that they have discovered that it is absolutely a fact that they have become more than conquerors "through him that loved us."

Chapter Four

Conscience and the Sense of Guilt

An impressive line in Axel Munthe's book, *The Story of San Michele*, says, "A man can stand a lot as long as he can stand himself. He can live without hope, without books, without friends, without music as long as he can listen to his own thoughts." Because this is so patently true, the wise thing, the absolutely necessary thing for every man is to cultivate at all costs a self with which he can live in peace and happiness. He must look to his conscience and eradicate the sense of guilt.

One thing is sure, whether you like it or not, you have to live with yourself. Goethe once said, "Beloved brother, let us not forget that a man can never get away from himself."

Lord Byron, when fleeing from England, heartbrokenly asked: "What exile from himself can flee?"

Indeed, it is a fact that a man may flee from other men and from familiar scenes and the obligations of life, and may even become a recluse in an obscure corner of the earth, he may turn his back on the social conventions and on early training and beliefs, but from himself there is no escape. I saw in a newspaper an account of a young man who was attempting to flee after having done a great wrong. He traveled the world over, but finally said this pathetic thing, "Everywhere I go I am still myself, and I myself am the penalty for the wrong I have done."

This is one of the inescapable facts of life—you have to live with what you are. For some this may be described as heaven; for others, it is literally hell. For some it is romance; for others it is intolerable boredom. In some men happiness and delight well up out of their hearts. They are alive and vibrant with the sheer joy of living. Life for them is an ever-fresh adventure. Every morning means a fresh beginning, every evening brings the deep satisfaction of a day richly lived. Such men are constantly finding within themselves unexplored riches and fresh sources of happiness. It is a joy to live with a self like that.

There are other men for whom it is not so. They have divided and conflicting personalities. In them is a contentious internecine spirit. They are at odds with themselves most of the time. They are like one of the characters in a modern novel about whom the author says, "He was not a personality, he was a civil war." Theirs is a self which desires to do right, but all too readily acquiesces in evil. Theirs is a self stung by remorse and haunted by a sense of guilt over past misdeeds. Theirs is a self which is horribly conscious of self because it is concerned only with self. To live with a self like that is hell. Nor is there any evasion, any escape. We have to live with what we are.

In the light of this grace and inescapable fact it becomes evident that the supremely important thing is to develop a self with which we can live satisfactorily. Since whether we like it or not we do have to live with ourselves, we profoundly want to become good company for ourselves. Each of us wants to be able to enjoy the self we have to live with.

The soul becomes apparent only as it develops. We are continuously building up or breaking down the self with which we were born. Through the years every thought, every emotion, every experience contributes to the quality of the self. No matter how old we are, or how set we may be, our self is in the making. We are all in the continuous process of creating the self we have to live with. Everything contributes to its greatness or littleness. You will remember Tennyson's discerning remark, "I am part of all I have met." By the same token everything we have met is part of us.

Winfred Rhodes, the helpful writer, expressed it in a great phrase, "Life's greatest achievement is the continual remaking of your self so that at last you know how to live." This constant process of self-development is expressed in such everyday remarks as: "How he has grown!" or "He is not the man he used to be."

These remarks represent a statement of the fact that we are constantly developing, whether for good or bad.

How go about developing a self we can live with happily, a self free from the domination of a wounded conscience and carrying a sense of guilt? We could indulge in much theory and speculation at this point, but a more effective method is to analyze an actual specimen in the laboratory of life. Let us take a man who had tremendous difficulty living with himself, but who solved the problem so effectively that he became one of the greatest men of all time. He is the eminent thinker, philosopher, and leader in the Christian Church, Paul, the apostle. He was a man who, by his own admission, suffered acute inner conflict and division. He once cried, "O wretched man that I am! Who shall deliver me from the body of this death?"

That is a very graphic description of inner conflict. He evidently had trouble with his good intentions too, for he complained that "The good that I would I do not: but the evil which I would not, that I do." But he won his fight with himself, and finally at the end of a life of heroic proportions, great in achievement but studded with pain, shipwreck, stonings, beatings, and prison, ending in martyrdom, he was able to say: "I have fought a good fight, I have finished my course, I have kept the faith." The man who said that was a man at peace with himself, who had developed a self with which he could live with profound inner contentment.

And what was his secret? It is expressed in these words, without which no explanation of this great life is possible: "I live; yet not I, but Christ liveth in me." That is to say, his life was now centered not in his divided and inharmonious personality, but in Christ, in whom are no divisions nor conflicts. Christ became the center around which his personality organized itself, and so the divisions in Paul's personality were healed and he became a self with whom it was pleasant for him to live.

Psychiatrists are now saying what the ministers have always said, that a clear mind, free of, or forgiven for, wrongdoing, is essential to the harmonious organization of a man's personality. Marcus Aurelius, one of the world's wisest men, knew the truth of these things. "The one thing worth living for," he declared, "is to keep one's soul pure."

The right may also be determined on the basis of results. Is wrong workable? Is it sensible? Seneca wisely declared, "If thou wouldst bring all things under subjection, subject thyself to reason." Jesus said to the man who sinned, "Thou fool, this night thy soul shall be required of thee."

Men afterward say, "I was a fool to have done that." It is not "the morning after" that is most tragic but "the years afterward."

A good skill to develop is a capacity for moral previewing, the ability to foresee the result; to project the mind ahead and see how a thing will look after it is done. A man thinking about committing a sin would do well to practice reading about it as if it had afterward become public.

The first function of religion, and I believe of psychiatry too, is to point the way to happier lives by teaching men and women how to cope with a sense of guilt which is due to their own unwisdom.

Psychiatry uses its own method of diagnosis and treatment.

Religion brings to distressed minds the knowledge of God's forgiveness and thus of the peace that passeth all understanding.

Chapter Five

Self-Criticism, Failure, and Success

A distinguished statesman said that in his youth he heard one sentence which, through the later years, had done him no end of good. He has, he declared, repeated it frequently all his adult life, and it has proved a marvelous source of strength. The sentence is: "You can become strongest in your weakest place."

It is a good sentence and states two important things about you and me. First, it calls attention to the obvious fact that we have weak places and a weakest place. Of course we do not like to admit that fact; we prefer to dwell on our strong points. We do not like to be honest with ourselves.

It is not easy to be absolutely honest with ourselves owing to what psychiatrists call rationalization. That is, we have a tendency not to be objective in our attitude toward ourselves. We set our minds to work, not upon dealing with the facts as they are, but upon inventing rational reasons for our courses of conduct. Our unconscious minds play tricks on us, and unless we watch our minds they will deceive us, keeping us from being entirely honest with ourselves, from realizing that we have weak places.

Second, the sentence tells us that we can be strongest in our weakest place. It does not say that we may become merely strong in the places where we are now weak, but that we may become strongest in the place which is now our weakest spot. Some of the tribes of Africa believe that when one man vanquishes another, the strength of the vanquished passes into the victor and he thereby becomes that much stronger. When you conquer a weakness, the strength that lies in that weakness, its power over you, passes into you. Each time you overcome the weakness you acquire an additional part of its strength. Its strength is diminished with each victory and your strength is correspondingly increased.

The ultimate result is the complete destruction of your weakness and your acquisition of the strength it had over you. When we vigorously set ourselves to overcome a weakness which we recognize, the direct campaign which we wage tends to bring all of our forces into play at that point. We concentrate a great measure of strength at our weakest point, making it our strongest.

Let the process known as "welding" illustrate the thought. Welding is a process in which two pieces of metal are fused at their point of contact, making a joint that is usually stronger than the parent metal itself. Intense heat is applied at the point of contact. The intense heat and resulting fusion makes the point that was weak stronger than any other.

We should keep in mind that the tendency of our personality is to palliate, to excuse and to defend our weaknesses. At times we need to be jarred out of ourselves, so as to see ourselves with such distinctness that our minds will be forced to honestly accept the fact of our woeful weakness. Holding this realization firmly in mind, attack your weakest place with determination and it will become your strongest place.

Here is an example from everyday life of the operation of the power of faith. A young man came to see me and said he had an insatiable appetite for alcohol which was fast destroying his effectiveness in business. His craving was so great that several times he had arisen in the middle of the night to get himself a drink. A psychiatrist would probably have diagnosed his case as "the will to fail,"—that is, that, basically, he wanted to fail. That is not infrequently the correct assumption in such cases. He wanted me to pray with him, comfort him, and urge him to go out and fight a fight which he confidently expected to lose, and then, having failed, come back for more prayer and more comfort. After he did just that several times, I told him there was no use trying and advised him not to try. He was amazed at this, and I explained that the gospel really does not urge us to try harder, but to believe harder. If the gospel did otherwise, it would be only for those of strong will. The only fight it urges is the fight of faith, the struggle to believe.

I assured him that however much he stirred up his will to succeed, he would probably fail because he visualized himself as failing. His will might heroically declare, "I will," but at the same time his imagination whispered, "I cannot." And because imagination is stronger than will, his will would lose. He needed to imagine himself not to be failing but winning. His faith needed to paint that picture firmly on his inner consciousness. So I asked him to believe by an act of pure faith that he would vanquish his craving—not tomorrow, or sometime in the future, but to believe that by the grace of God he was that very minute freed from its domination.

"According to your faith, be it done unto you," said Christ. He asked me if I was certain of that, and I assured him that I was. By an act of faith he accepted the idea, and whatever were the mental operations involved in the process, the fact remains that at the end of the month he told me he had not had the slightest desire for alcohol. Now, at the end of a year and a half he has had no recurrence of the desire. The moral lesion was healed by so great a curative force that no vestige of diseased tissue remains. What fruitless struggle could not do was accomplished by the tremendous power of faith in Christ. Any problem of this life can be successfully handled if by faith we merely open our minds to the power of God.

CHAPTER SIX

Grief and Sorrow

Some years ago I had a friend, a great soul. He was a big man, big physically and big of heart. One stormy night his home telephone rang and at the other end was the agonized voice of an acquaintance who had just had great tragedy come to him. It was one of the most terrible tragedies that can happen to a man, the discovery of the infidelity of a beloved wife. She had gone, left his home. He was alone in the dawning knowledge that her love was a broken thing. Piteously, like a child in the dark, his heart dead within him, he called my friend over the telephone. My friend immediately got out his car, drove for a good many miles through the storm to this man's home, and found him bowed in hopeless grief. My friend walked in without a word, went up to the broken man, put his great arms about him, pulled him up close and said, "Come with me."

They gathered up a few of his belongings and got into the tight little car where the man sat with his shoulder pressed against my big bulky friend. The stricken man told me, afterward, that as they drove through the night not a word was spoken. What could be said? The unspoken attitude of human sympathy had to speak the message, and he said that as he looked upon the strong, kindly face of his friend, lighted by the dim glow of the dash light, and reflected in the windshield, there came over him a great sense of peace and protection and calm comfort. My friend had thrown his tabernacle over him. So God, who loves us with an infinite love, has spread his tabernacle over our dear departed loved ones.

Death has always been pictured as a dark angel, as a sinister figure. I wonder if the metaphor of going home to a mother, to a father, isn't a better and more accurate one. I know a man who, in the struggle in these difficult days in the heart of a great city, became overwhelmed with trouble. He is a strong, resourceful man, but life hit him many blows, and the going became exceedingly hard. He felt a deep and irresistible desire to go back to his boyhood home and have a visit with his aged mother.

He wanted, somehow, to recapture the enthusiasm and zest of life which had been drained from his spirit. Streaks of gray were beginning to show in his hair, and as Charles Lamb once said, "Our spirits grow gray before our hair," so it was with this man.

He told me afterward that he went back to the old home, and his mother, like mothers in every age and in every place, wanted to feed him, give him a good dinner such as he used to have. She put food and drink before him and talked to him about old-fashioned, intimate family matters. She was slaking his thirst, and feeding the deeper hunger of his life. As he sat at the table, as she passed by, she put her hands, soft and tender and wrinkled, on his head as if she knew the burden he carried and the pain in his heart, and was trying as only a mother can to wipe away the tears from his eyes.

He said that in the quietness of that place peace came over him and a new enthusiasm for living came stealing back into his heart. What we often find in a mother or in a loving father here on earth, our dead have found in the great mother heart, in the great father heart of God. Their eyes, closed in death, have opened in the light of an eternal home.

So I say to you who mourn, that if we are to believe the Scriptures, and I know that we can believe them, we may be sure that those whom we have "loved long since and lost awhile" are happy and peaceful and contented, for they are in the Father's house and the Father is with them.

Jesus once said, "In my Father's house are many mansions: If it were *not so*, I would have told you. I go to prepare a place for you, . . . that where I am, there ye may be also." He is there, and wherever he is cannot be other than a place of beauty and happiness and peace. Thus sorrow is lifted by our faith in the goodness of God.

But there is another and profound source of grief which we must consider. It is very common and is subtle, for the average person does not think of it as a deep grief resting upon the spirit, subtracting from life its color and enjoyment. Deep-centered grief often emanates from a loss of ideas and of faith.

Many people are trying to satisfy deep hungers and do not know how to do it. The only way that has occurred to some is loose living, compromised morality, and even dissipation. But apparently that method is proving a sad disappointment, for in ever-increasing numbers, people, and particularly younger people—for they are still honest and frank—are turning to religious experience as the only sure antidote for redundant boredom. Here is a generation in confusion, which has lost its way, not only with regard to its collective economic and social life, but also in its individual life. It may be said that multitudes have "come to grief" because their ideals have been lost.

What is the answer to this tragic condition? There is only one thinker who has the answer, the wisest man who ever lived, a man named Jesus Christ. What does he have to say? He says, and the statement shows magnificent insight, uncanny genius: "The kingdom of God is within you." What did he mean by that?

In each of us is God. If we reject him, he is still there in us just the same, for he never rejects us. But unless we give him control of our inward life he can do little for us. Weak as we are, we have the power to render the God in us ineffective. The minute a man says with sincerity to God within him, "you take control," that very minute he realizes the kingdom of God within him, and radiant life begins for him. The secret of happiness lies in exercising the spiritual power within yourself. Simply say with a whole heart: "God, you are in me—dominate me," and presently your life is at springtime, radiant and beautiful. When Jesus Christ says, "the kingdom of God is within you," he is saying what wise men have always said, namely, that in you yourself is the answer to your own happiness. This is the antidote to deep inward grief of the spirit.

CHAPTER SEVEN

The Company of the Lonely

In compiling a list of the world's greatest novels an eminent professor of literature gave first place to that thrilling old classic, *Robinson Crusoe* by Daniel Defoe. He justified giving the primacy to this book on the ground that not only is it the first English novel, but it is wrought, as every great novel must be, out of a fundamental fact of human experience. A great novel must deal with a profound truth about life. This *Robinson Crusoe* does with surpassing genius.

It portrays a man fallen upon a most terrible fate—that of loneliness. The highlight of the book which stirs every reader is where the cure for that loneliness is found. Every day Crusoe comes to his lookout point, where he has rigged up a cloth at the top of a pole. He stands gazing across the sea, hands shading his eyes, searching for white sails against the empty horizon.

Standing there in his tatters, skin bronzed, hair long and unkempt, the beach grass waving at his feet, utterly alone, he is a tragic figure. He longs for the touch of a human hand, the sound of a human voice, and the friendly light on a human face. His solitary vigil once again unrewarded, he turns to go but stops short, in wild surprise, for before him in the sands of his supposedly desert island is an unmistakable human footprint, not his own.

In a manner usually less dramatic but no less poignant, every man in the long voyage of the years is likely to find himself like Crusoe upon some lonely island of the spirit. Indeed, there is a fundamental loneliness which haunts all who think deeply upon human experience. Man, at birth, enters this world alone from out the vast silences. Here he comes to be closely bound to others by strong ties of love and friendship. Yet in him remains a mystic homesickness, as if he does not really belong here but is, as an old hymn says, "A pilgrim and a stranger." Literature, art, and music, man's means of expressing himself, give utterance to this cosmic loneliness.

Sculptors, painters, and writers have given us the thought that we are not detached spirits, each living his allotted three score and ten, but elements in the ceaseless flow of eternity. Sir James Jeans, the eminent scientist, touched on the same thought when he said, "It may be that each individual consciousness is a brain cell in a universal mind." We do not live, according to Jeans, as distinct entities for a limited moment of time but tarry on earth during what is called human life, passing on finally, not to extinction, as though our purpose were accomplished, but to further functioning in other capacities in the never-ending process of cosmic mind of which each of us is a constituent part. It is a noble thought and may explain that vague loneliness which the thoughtful man feels now and then as though somehow he did not really belong here but felt the pull of some mystic homeland ever drawing his restless feet toward it.

My experience as a pastor has clearly shown me that a genuine Christian is never a victim of loneliness. Mark you, I said a genuine Christian, and that, of course, does not mean everyone who goes to church and glibly recites the creeds. A genuine Christian is one who sincerely tries to live in the spirit of Christ, has a simple trust and who has mastered the workable techniques of faith. This type of Christian has a friendly and sympathetic attitude toward all men. He is kindly in his relationships, and possesses a generous spirit, which is well able to lift him above everyday frictions. Moreover, he has learned to cope with shyness and oversensitiveness, because he has conquered the ego centeredness which causes them. The Christlike spirit that actuates him makes him too big for that carping pettiness which destroys friendship, leaving us forsaken and alone.

Another thing I have noticed about the genuine Christian is that though he may be compelled by circumstances to be much alone, he is not lonely, for he has inner resources to draw upon and consequently always finds himself in good company. As a man playing solitaire whiles away the lonely hours pleasantly because he enjoys his own game, so the man with worthwhile things in his own mind can play life's game in solitary because he is interesting even to himself. The important factor is what is in a man's mind.

Many people never read anything worthwhile; some never read at all, save the newspaper headlines. The extent of this indifference to good reading is evidenced by the astonishing prevalence of picture publications. The person who stocks his mind with great thought lays up treasures and resources upon which he may live happily, finding himself interesting enough to make loneliness impossible.

Faith is the answer to the problem of loneliness. As a pastor I have seen evidence of this assertion too many times to have any doubt about it. Consider the loneliness of bereavement. A loved one has been taken by death. For a while the reaction is one of lonesomeness, the agony of separation. The bereaved one misses the object of his love withal the pain of grief. The danger is that the grief may become abnormal through the withdrawal of one's love into oneself and through a spirit of bitterness toward an unkind world. There are thousands of people today whose lives are disintegrating because they have not developed enough faith to cope with the sorrow that is breaking down their personalities.

The man of faith, although he suffers all the pain of loss, at the same time believes that "all things work together for good to them that love God." He believes that the soul is immortal and that God is a Being with absolute love in his heart. He turns to God for comfort, and God does not disappoint him. If his faith is strong enough, it makes his consciousness of the Divine compassion and protection so complete that loneliness vanishes and a sense of companionship takes its place.

An old Russian proverb says, "The hammer shatters glass, but forges steel." Some people are like glass—the hammer of circumstance breaks them in pieces. Other people are like steel—the hammer strikes and instead of breaking them, forges them into new forms of strength and beauty. Christianity puts the steel-like element in people, so that they do not break under the hammers of circumstance. That precious ingredient is given them by faith.

Chapter Eight

Love and Marriage

I believe any man and wife can make a success of their marriage if they enter upon it with a spiritual attitude. I advise couples to pray together the first night of their marriage and every night thereafter. I know scores of present-day young couples who say grace at meals and many more who frequently read together from the Bible. These marriages do not break. They are cemented by the greatest power in the world—faith in God.

I have seen many failing marriages saved and permanently restored when both or even one of the partners was willing to bring religion into the situation.

A young woman came to me and said she and her husband had reached the breaking point. Misunderstandings had grown to enormous proportions and frequent differences had become hateful and bitter quarreling. She was about ready for the divorce court, she said, and from what I gathered he felt the same way. But she had a sensitive conscience about divorce, and, besides, down deep, as it later appeared, she still loved her husband and, of course, wanted to save their marriage.

"Have you, as a minister, any suggestion to make?" she asked.

"Yes, I have a suggestion," I replied. "I have known it to work in other cases like yours, and, in fact, it will work in any situation if it is faithfully tried."

"What is it?" she demanded, half skeptical, half hopeful.

"Pray with your husband," I said. "Go home and get him to kneel down and pray with you."

"Oh," she answered, her face fallen with disappointment, "I couldn't do that. He would make fun of me. We used to pray together every night, when we were first married, but we gave that up long ago."

"It will work," I replied. "I want you to promise you will pray with him tonight."

She did not say she would, but the next day she was back again as radiant a young woman as I ever saw. She fairly bubbled over with excitement and joy as she told me how she had struggled all evening for courage to make the suggestion to her husband, sunk behind his paper.

Finally she went over to him and said, "Jim, we can't seem to get together any other way, and all our arguments don't get us anywhere, and, Jim, in spite of everything, I really love you. Will you do one thing for me—will you—will you pray with me like we used to?"

She said he looked at her rather strangely.

"And then what do you think he said?" she asked. "He said, 'I thought of that a couple of times myself, but I didn't have the nerve to suggest it.'"

"Why," she cried, "it was wonderful, unbelievable; we got down on our knees as we did when we were first married and we talked to God like a couple of children, and all the trouble seemed to melt away all at once."

"Keep it up," I urged her, "and you will hold that refound happiness."

Religion works when used in human relationships. If you want happiness in marriage—and, of course, you do—practice your religion, and if your husband or wife will not join you in prayer and faith, then do all the praying yourself. One person with real faith can bring to bear a spiritual force sufficient to destroy irritating differences. Faith is so potent that one partner can lift both to that higher level where understanding and unity are attained.

Chapter Nine
The Faith That Heals

Many miracles of prayer and faith are taking place today in the field of physical and mental health.

This was once a very important aspect of Christianity. The New Testament is full of accounts of healing by Christ and his disciples. The tendency of the Christian religion under the influence of our era's naturalistic-scientific zeal has been to ignore its healing element. But now that science is becoming more mature, and its real harmony with religion better established, it is becoming evident that even as science has set free forces in the material world, so a more scientific application of prayer and faith tends to set free once more the healing forces such as are described in the New Testament as being of usual occurrence. There is now, I feel, a happy tendency by psychiatry, and general medicine, and surgery to work together with religion, each in its own realm to be sure, but with sympathy and understanding, in the common cause of healing body, mind and soul.

One doctor put it very well: "I treated my patient and God healed her." If we will avail ourselves of the best that medical science can give us and at the same time by faith and prayer put ourselves in the hands of God, being sure to pray always that God's will be done whatever that may involve, we shall be the object of curative and restorative forces of remarkable efficacy. The head of the medical service in a great university hospital said, "One should send for his minister as he sends for his doctor when he becomes ill." That is to say that God helps the sick in two ways, through the science of medicine and surgery, and through the science of faith and prayer. This latter brings the mind and spirit of the sick into harmony with God so that his healing power may operate. The physician thereby receives a superb cooperation.

My brother, Dr. Robert C. Peale, a physician and surgeon, says: "Because of the abiding faith and trust in the Almighty of the injured or sick person, I constantly see, as a surgeon, recoveries that were thought impossible. I also see poor results because of an attempted cure by religion or science alone. I have therefore become convinced that there is a definite and fixed relationship between religion and science and that God has given us both as weapons against disease and unhappiness. Used together for the benefit of mankind, their possibilities are unlimited, separately they can only be of limited benefit."

Simple faith in God opens our lives in an amazing manner to the forces of healing and strength and growth. All serious students of mankind know that man's essential quality is not physical or material but spiritual. A man can live a purely physical and material life for a while, but he will be beaten eventually, because he has cut himself off from the source of life-giving vitality. Like a pool of water separated from the living waters of a running stream he presently becomes unhealthy. Life is unhappy and sinful because it is cut off from the flow of life-giving force. Simple faith and surrender to God correct this condition. It is remarkable what a sincere attempt to harmonize our lives with God's power will do physically, mentally, and spiritually.

If we only believe, there is no limit to the blessings God will give us. We are told that Christ came to give us an abundant life. That means something far beyond the narrow, limited, frustrated lives most of us live. The whole emphasis of the New Testament which we so tragically miss is that God wants to pour out blessings in overflowing generosity. No blessing is too great, no power too strong, no victory too complete. All is ours.

About the Author

Norman Vincent Peale (1898–1993) was among the most influential and prolific ministers of the twentieth century. His worldwide classic *The Power of Positive Thinking*, published in 1952, revolutionized the field of self-help and practical spirituality, and it popularized mystical themes of mind-power metaphysics throughout the world.

The Power
of Awareness

THE POWER OF AWARENESS

*The Extraordinary Guide
to Your Limitless Potential—
Now in a Special Condensation*

by Neville

Contents

INTRODUCTION
Doer of the Word *by Mitch Horowitz*   79

1. Consciousness   83

2. Power of Assumption   85

3. Desire   88

4. The Truth That Sets You Free   89

5. Attention   90

6. Renunciation   92

7. Preparing Your Place   93

8. Creation   94

9. Subjective Control   96

10. Acceptance   97

11. Effortless Way   98

12. Essentials   99

13. Free Will   102

14. Failure   104

15. Destiny   107

About the Author   109

Introduction

Doer of the Word

by Mitch Horowitz

The Power of Awareness is, in many respects, the perfect Neville book. The mystic wrote it in full bloom of his abilities as an author and speaker. The book sums up Neville's philosophy of creative imagination with exquisite clarity—indeed *The Power of Awareness* makes me think that of all the writers to emerge from the American metaphysical scene in the last century, Neville was the most elegant as a literary figure and communicator. (In this regard, he's closely rivaled by Alan Watts.)

The book's essential point is that you are a composite of exactly *what you believe to be true about yourself.* Your persistently held assumptions and mental pictures *are* your destiny, more than any past event or present circumstance. This is a message of extraordinary self-liberation.

It is also a deeply challenging message, especially for those experiencing health difficulties or physical maladies.

Are such things really malleable to a change of mentality? And, in the face of chronic pain or other tactilely felt conditions, is a change in psyche even possible?

These are areas for the reader to experiment with. It is possible that in order to experience the full sway of our mental powers we must begin with conditions that we feel we can more readily effect, and watch for changes to arrive through already established channels, before moving on to more ambitious aims. It is also possible, as I explore in *The Miracle Club*, that we may be unable to experience, from within our present mentality, the ultimate role of awareness as the shaper of reality. But this should not serve as a deterrent to our personal experiments. Extraordinary events *do* occur, large and small, and Neville urges us to probe such occurrences for correlation between sustained mental picture and outer activity.

Every one of us lives by assumptions, whether or not we acknowledge them. We all harbor untested, psychologically conditioned, and second-hand notions about life, which we seldom scrutinize. Acknowledging that this is so gives us remarkable freedom to select and road-test new personal philosophies and approaches. That is the spirit in which I hope you will approach this book. You have everything to gain by embracing your freedom to experiment with a new inner creed. That is what Neville offers.

One of Neville's traits that I most love is his continual challenge to the reader or listener to simply *try*. To test his ideas, this very minute, and see if they do not bring results.

If not, he urges, forget all about me; but if so then dig deeper.

I want to add on a personal note that you will not be alone in these experiments. I and many others who love Neville's work are laboring with you. I hold a deep conviction that not only was Neville the most beautiful writer and speaker to emerge from the American metaphysical scene in the last century, but that he also conveyed ideas of remarkable and mysterious truth. These ideas will not simply disclose themselves on the page or through a speaker's voice, however. They require application and perseverance. You will likely encounter tantalizing successes and, at times, dispiriting failures, a topic that Neville addresses forthrightly in one of the last chapters in this book.

My hope is that this condensation *The Power of Awareness* will provide you with a springboard to action, and with a lesson plan that can be absorbed in a single sitting. And after you take it in, become, as Neville and Scripture urges, a "doer of the Word." See what transpires.

*This book is to reveal your infinite power,
against which no earthly
force is of the slightest significance.
It is to show you who you are,
your purpose and your destiny.*

1. Consciousness

It is only by a change of consciousness, by actually changing your concept of yourself that you can "build more stately mansions"—the manifestations of higher and higher concepts. (By manifesting is meant experiencing the results of these concepts in your world). It is of vital importance to understand clearly just what consciousness is.

The reason lies in the fact that *consciousness is the one and only reality, it is the first and only cause-substance of the phenomena of life.* Nothing has existence for man save through the consciousness he has of it. Therefore, it is to consciousness you must turn, for it is the only foundation on which the phenomena of life can be explained.

If we accept the idea of a first cause, it would follow that the evolution of that cause could never result in anything foreign to itself. That is, if the first cause-substance is light, all its evolutions, fruits and manifestations would remain light. The first cause-substance being consciousness, all its evolutions, fruits and phenomena must remain consciousness. All that could be observed would be a higher or lower form or variation of the same thing. In other words, if your consciousness is the only reality, it must also be the *only* substance. Consequently, what appears to you as circumstances, conditions and even material objects are really only the products of your own consciousness. Nature, then, as a thing or a complex of things external to your mind, must be rejected. You and your environment cannot be regarded as existing separately. You and your world are *one*.

Therefore, you must turn from the objective appearance of things to the *subjective center* of things, your consciousness, if you truly desire to know the cause of the phenomena of life, and how to use this knowledge to realize your fondest dreams. In the midst of the apparent contradictions, antagonisms and contrasts of your life, *there is only one principle at work*, only your consciousness operating. Difference does not consist in variety of substance, but in variety of arrangement of the same cause-substance, your consciousness.

The world moves with motiveless necessity. By this is meant that it has no motive of its own, but is under the necessity of manifesting your concept, the arrangement of your mind, and *your mind is always arranged in the image of all you believe and consent to as true*. The rich man, poor man, beggar man or thief are not different minds, but different arrangements of the same mind, in the same sense that a piece of steel when magnetized differs not in substance from its demagnetized state but in the arrangement and order of its molecules. A single electron revolving in a specified orbit constitutes the unit of magnetism. When a piece of steel or anything else is demagnetized, the revolving electrons have not stopped. Therefore, the magnetism has not gone out of existence. There is only a rearrangement of the particles, so that they produce no outside or perceptible effect. When particles are arranged at random, mixed up in all directions, the substance is said to be demagnetized; but when particles are marshalled in ranks so that a number of them face in one direction, the substance is a magnet. Magnetism is not generated; it is displayed. *Health, wealth, beauty and genius are not created; they are only manifested* by the arrangement of your mind—that is, by your concept of yourself. The importance of this in your daily life should be immediately apparent.

The basic nature of the primal cause is consciousness. Therefore, the ultimate substance of all things is *consciousness*.

2. Power of Assumption

Man's chief delusion is his conviction that there are *causes other than his own state of consciousness*. All that befalls a man—all that comes from him—happens as a result of his state of consciousness. A man's consciousness is all that he thinks and desires and loves, all that he believes is true and consents to. That is why a change of consciousness is necessary before you can change your outer world.

"Be ye transformed by the renewing of your mind."

To be transformed, the whole basis of your thoughts must change. But your thoughts cannot change unless you have *new ideas*, for you think from your ideas. All transformation begins with an intense, burning desire to be transformed. The first step in the 'renewing of the mind' is *desire*. You must want to be different before you can begin to change yourself. Then you must *make your future dream a present fact*. You do this by *assuming the feeling of your wish fulfilled*. By desiring to be other than what you are, you can create an ideal of the person you want to be and *assume that you are already that person*. If this assumption is persisted in until it becomes your dominant feeling, the attainment of your ideal is inevitable. The ideal you hope to achieve is always ready for an incarnation, but unless you yourself offer it human parentage it is incapable of birth. Therefore, your attitude should be one in which—having desired to express a higher state—you alone accept the task of incarnating this new and greater value of yourself.

In giving birth to your ideal you must bear in mind that the methods of mental and spiritual knowledge are entirely different. This is a point that is truly understood by probably not more than one person in a million. You know a thing mentally by looking at it from the outside, by comparing it with other things, by analyzing it and defining it; whereas you can know a thing spiritually only by becoming it. You must be the thing itself and not merely talk about it or look at it.

Just as the moth in his desire to know the flame was willing to destroy himself, so must you in becoming a new person be willing to die to your present self.

You must be conscious of *being* healthy if you are to know what health is. You must be conscious of *being* secure if you are to know what security is. Therefore, to incarnate a new and greater value of yourself, you must assume that you already are what you want to be and then live by faith in this assumption—which is not yet incarnate in the body of your life—in confidence that this new value or state of consciousness will become incarnated through your absolute fidelity to the assumption that you are that which you desire to be. This is what wholeness means, what integrity means. They mean submission of the whole self to the feeling of the wish fulfilled in certainty that that new state of consciousness is the renewing of mind which transforms.

Imagination is the only redemptive power in the universe. However, your nature is such that it is optional to you whether you remain in your present concept of yourself (a hungry being longing for freedom, health and security) or choose to become the instrument of your own redemption, imagining yourself as that which you want to be, and thereby satisfying your hunger and redeeming yourself.

3. Desire

The changes which take place in your life *as a result of your changed concept of yourself* always appear to the unenlightened to be the result, not of a change of your consciousness, but of chance, outer cause or coincidence. However, the only fate governing your life is the fate determined by your own concepts, your own assumptions; for an assumption, *though false*, if persisted in will harden into fact. The ideal you seek and hope to attain will not manifest itself, will not be realized by you, until you have imagined that you are already that ideal. There is no escape for you except by a radical psychological transformation of yourself, except by your assumption of the feeling of your wish fulfilled. Therefore, make results or accomplishments the crucial test of your ability to use your imagination.

Everything depends on your attitude towards yourself. *That which you will not affirm as true of yourself can never be realized by you* for that attitude alone is the necessary condition by which you realize your goal.

You must imagine that you are already experiencing what you desire. That is, you must assume the feeling of the fulfillment of your desire until you are possessed by it and this feeling crowds all other ideas out of your consciousness.

If you do not believe that you are He (the person you want to be) then you remain as you are. Through the faithful systematic cultivation of the feeling of the wish fulfilled, *desire becomes the promise of its own fulfillment.* The assumption of the feeling of the wish fulfilled makes the future dream a present fact.

4. The Truth That Sets You Free

The drama of life is a psychological one in which all the conditions, circumstances and events of your life are brought to pass by your assumptions.

Since your life is determined by your assumptions you are forced to recognize the fact that you are either a slave to your assumptions or their master. To become the master of your assumptions is the key to undreamed of freedom and happiness. You can attain this mastery by deliberate conscious control of your imagination. You determine your assumptions in this way: Form a mental image, a picture of the state desired, of the person you want to be. Concentrate your attention upon the feeling that you are already that person. First, visualize the picture in your consciousness. Then *feel* yourself to be in that state as though it actually formed your surrounding world. By your imagination that which was a mere mental image is changed into a seemingly solid reality.

The great secret is a controlled imagination and a well sustained attention firmly and repeatedly focused on the object to be accomplished. It cannot be emphasized too much that, by creating an ideal within your mental sphere, by assuming that you are already that ideal, *you identify yourself with it and thereby transform yourself into its image.* This was called by the ancient teachers, "Subjection to the will of God" or "Resting in the Lord", and the only true test of "Resting in the Lord" is that all who *do* rest are inevitably transformed into the image of that in which they rest. You become according to your resigned will, and your resigned will is your concept of yourself and all that you consent to and accept as true. You, assuming the feeling of your wish fulfilled and continuing therein, take upon yourself the results of that state; not assuming the feeling of your wish fulfilled, you are ever free of the results.

5. Attention

Attention is forceful in proportion to the narrowness of its focus, that is, when it is obsessed with a single idea or sensation. It is steadied and powerfully focused only by such an adjustment of the mind as permits you to see one thing only, for you steady the attention and increase its power by confining it. *The desire which realizes itself is always a desire upon which attention is exclusively concentrated,* for an idea is endowed with power only in proportion to the degree of attention fixed on it. Concentrated observation is the attentive attitude directed towards some specific end. The attentive attitude involves selection, for when you pay attention it signifies that you have decided to focus your attention on one object or state rather than on another.

Therefore, when you know what you want you must deliberately focus your attention on the feeling of your wish fulfilled until that feeling fills the mind and crowds all other ideas out of consciousness.

The power of attention is the measure of your inner force. Concentrated observation of one thing shuts out other things and causes them to disappear. *The great secret of success is to focus the attention on the feeling of the wish fulfilled without permitting any distraction.* All progress depends upon an *increase* of attention.

To aid in mastering the control of your attention practice this exercise. Night after night, just before you drift off to sleep, strive to hold your attention on the activities of the day *in reverse order*. Focus your attention on the last thing you did, that is, getting *in* to bed and then move it backward in time over the events until you reach the first event of the day, getting *out* of bed. This is no easy exercise, but just as specific exercises greatly help in developing specific muscles, this will greatly help in developing the "muscle" of your attention. Your attention must be developed, controlled and concentrated in order to change your concept of yourself successfully and thereby change your future. Imagination is able to do anything *but only according to the internal direction of your attention*.

When you attain control of the internal direction of your attention, you will no longer stand in shallow water but will launch out into the deep of life. You will walk in the assumption of the wish fulfilled as on a foundation more solid even than earth.

6. Renunciation

There is a great difference between *resisting evil and renouncing it.*

When you resist evil, you give it your attention, you continue to make it real. When you renounce evil you take your attention from it and give your attention to what you want. Now is the time to control your imagination and

> *"Give beauty for ashes, joy for mourning, praise for the spirit of heaviness, that they might be called trees of righteousness, the planting of the Lord that He might be glorified."*

You give beauty for ashes when you concentrate your attention on things as you would like them to be rather than on things as they are. You give joy for mourning when you maintain a joyous attitude regardless of unfavorable circumstances. You give praise for the spirit of heaviness when you maintain a confident attitude instead of succumbing to despondency. In this quotation the Bible uses the word tree as a synonym for man. You become a tree of righteousness when the above mental states are a permanent part of your consciousness.

7. Preparing Your Place

All is yours. Do not go seeking for that which you are. Appropriate it, claim it, assume it. *Everything* depends upon your concept of yourself. That which you do not claim as true of yourself, cannot be realized by you. The promise is

> *"Whosoever hath, to him it shall be given, and he shall have more abundance; but whosoever hath not, from him shall be taken away even that which he seemeth to have."*

Hold fast, in your imagination, to all that is lovely and of good report for the lovely and the good are essential in your life if it is to be worthwhile. Assume it. You do this by imagining that you *already are* what you want to be—and *already have* what you want to have.

> *"As a man thinketh in his heart so is he."*

Be still and know that you are that which you desire to be, and you will never have to search for it.

In spite of your appearance of freedom of action, you obey, as everything else does, the law of assumption. Whatever you may think of the question of free will, the truth is *your experiences throughout your life are determined by your assumptions*—whether conscious or unconscious. An assumption *builds a bridge of incidents that lead inevitably to the fulfillment of itself.*

Man believes the future to be the natural development of the past. But the law of assumption clearly shows that this is not the case. Your assumption places you psychologically where you are not *physically*; then your senses pull you back from where you were psychologically to where you are physically. *It is these psychological forward motions that produce your physical forward motions in time.* Pre-cognition permeates all the scriptures of the world.

8. Creation

Creation is finished. Creativeness is only a deeper receptiveness, for the entire contents of all time and all space while experienced in a time sequence actually co-exist in an infinite and eternal now. In other words, all that you ever have been or ever will be—in fact, all that mankind ever was or ever will be, exists *now*. This is what is meant by creation and the statement that creation is finished means that nothing is ever to be created, it is only to be manifested. *What is called creativeness is only becoming aware of what already is.*

The whole of creation exists in you and it is your destiny to become increasingly aware of its infinite wonders and to experience ever greater and grander portions of it.

If creation is finished, and all events are taking place now, the question that springs naturally to the mind is "what determines your time track?" That is, what determines the events which you encounter? And the answer is *your concept of yourself.* Concepts determine the route that attention follows. Here is a good test to prove this fact. Assume the feeling of your wish fulfilled and observe the route that your attention follows. You will observe that as long as you remain faithful to your assumption, so long will your attention be confronted with images clearly related to that assumption. For example; if you assume that you have a wonderful business, you will notice how *in your imagination* your attention is focused on incident after incident relating to that assumption. Friends congratulate you, tell you how lucky you are. Others are envious and critical. From there your attention goes to larger offices, bigger bank balances and many other similarly related events. Persistence in this assumption will result in *actually experiencing in fact that which you assumed.*

The same is true regarding any concept. If your concept of yourself is that you are a failure you would encounter in your imagination a whole series of incidents in conformance to that concept.

9. Subjective Control

Your imagination is able to do all that you ask *in proportion to the degree of your attention.* All progress, all fulfillment of desire, depend upon the control and concentration of your attention.

Your attention is directed from within when you deliberately choose what you will be preoccupied with mentally. It is obvious that in the objective world your attention is not only attracted by but is constantly *directed* to external impressions. But, your control in the *subjective state* is almost non-existent, for in this state attention is usually the servant and not the master—the passenger and not the navigator—of your world. There is an enormous difference between attention directed objectively and attention directed subjectively, and the *capacity to change your future depends on the latter.* When you are able to control the movements of your attention in the subjective world you can modify or alter your life as you please. But this control cannot be achieved if you allow your attention to be attracted constantly from without. Each day, set yourself the task of deliberately withdrawing your attention from the objective world and of focusing it *subjectively.* In other words, concentrate on those thoughts or moods which you deliberately determine.

You will no longer accept the dominance of outside conditions or circumstances. You will not accept life on the basis of the world without. Having achieved control of the movements of your attention, and having discovered the mystery hid from the ages, that *Christ in you is your imagination*, you will assert the supremacy of *imagination* and put all things in subjection to it.

10. Acceptance

However much you seem to be living in a material world, *you are actually living in a world of imagination.*

Whenever you become completely absorbed in an emotional state you are at that moment assuming the feeling of the state fulfilled. If persisted in, whatsoever you are intensely emotional about you will experience in your world. These periods of absorption, of concentrated attention, are the beginnings of the things you harvest.

This shock reverses your time sense. By this is meant that *instead of your experience resulting from your past, it now becomes the result of being in imagination where you have not yet been physically.* In effect, this moves you across a bridge of incident to the physical realization of your imagined state. The man who at will can assume whatever state he pleases has found the keys to the Kingdom of Heaven. The keys are *desire, imagination and a steadily focused attention on the feeling of the wish fulfilled.*

Assume the spirit, the feeling of the wish fulfilled, and you will have opened the windows to receive the blessing. To assume a state is to get into the spirit of it. Your triumphs will be a surprise only to those who did not know your hidden passage from the state of longing to the assumption of the wish fulfilled.

The Lord of hosts will not respond to your wish until you have assumed the feeling of already being what you want to be, for *acceptance is the channel of His action.* Acceptance is the Lord of hosts in action.

11. The Effortless Way

The principle of 'Least Action' governs everything in physics from the path of a planet to the path of a pulse of light. Least Action is the minimum of energy, multiplied by the minimum of time. Therefore, in moving from your present state to the state desired, you must use the minimum of energy and take the shortest possible time. Your journey from one state of consciousness to another, is a psychological one, so, to make the journey you must employ the psychological equivalent of

'Least Action' and the psychological equivalent is mere assumption.

The day you fully realize the power of assumption, you discover that it works in complete conformity with this principle. It works by means of attention, minus effort. Thus, with least action through an assumption you hurry without haste and reach your goal without effort.

Because creation is finished, *what you desire already exists*. It is excluded from view because you can see only the contents of your own consciousness. It is the function of an assumption to call back the excluded view and restore full vision. *It is not the world but your assumptions that change.* An assumption brings the invisible into sight. It is nothing more nor less than seeing with the eye of God, i.e., imagination.

12. Essentials

The essential points in the successful use of the law of assumption are these: First, and above all, *yearning, longing, intense burning desire*. With all your heart you must want to be different from what you are. Intense, burning desire *is* the mainspring of action, the beginning of all successful ventures. In every great passion desire is concentrated.

> *"As the hart panteth after the water brooks, so panteth my soul after Thee, O God."*

> *"Blessed are they that hunger and thirst after righteousness for they shall be filled."*

Here the soul is interpreted as the sum total of all you believe, think, feel and accept as true; in other words, your present level of awareness. God means I AM, the source and fulfillment of all desire. This quotation describes how your present level of awareness longs to transcend itself. *Righteousness is the consciousness of already being what you want to be.*

Second, *cultivate physical immobility*, a physical incapacity not unlike the state described by Keats in his 'Ode to a Nightingale'.

> *"A drowsy numbness pains my senses, as though of hemlock I had drunk."*

It is a state akin to sleep, but one in which you are still in control of the direction of attention. You must learn to induce this state at will, but experience has taught that it is more easily induced after a substantial meal, or when you wake in the morning feeling very loath to arise. Then you are naturally disposed to enter this state. The value of physical immobility shows itself in the accumulation of mental force which absolute stillness brings with it. It increases your power of concentration.

"Be still and know that I am God."

In fact, the greater energies of the mind seldom break forth save when the body is stilled and the door of the senses closed to the objective world.

The third and last thing to do is to *experience in your imagination what you would experience in reality had you achieved your goal.* Imagine that you possess a quality or something you desire which hitherto has not been yours. Surrender yourself completely to this feeling until your whole being is possessed by it. This state differs from reverie in this respect: it is the result of a *controlled imagination and a steadied concentrated attention*, whereas reverie is the result of an uncontrolled imagination—usually just a daydream. In the controlled state, a minimum of effort suffices to keep your consciousness filled with the feeling of the wish fulfilled. The physical and mental immobility of this state is a powerful aid to voluntary attention and a major factor of minimum effort.

Apply these three points:
- Desire
- Physical immobility
- The assumption of the wish already fulfilled

This is the way to at-one-ment or *union with your objective.*

13. Free Will

The question is often asked, "what should be done between the assumption of the wish fulfilled and its realization?" *Nothing*. It is a delusion that, other than assuming the feeling of the wish fulfilled you can do anything to aid the realization of your desire. You think that you can do something, you want to do something; but, actually you can do nothing. *The illusion of the free will to do is but ignorance of the law of assumption* upon which all action is based. Everything happens automatically. All that befalls you, all that is done by you—*happens*. Your assumptions, *conscious or unconscious*, direct all thought and action to their fulfillment. To understand the law of assumption, to be convinced of its truth, means getting rid of all the illusions about free will to act. Free will actually means *freedom to select any idea you desire*. By assuming the idea *already* to be a fact, it is converted into reality. Beyond that, *free will ends* and everything happens in harmony with the concept assumed.

It is impossible to *do* anything. You must *be* in order to do.

If you had a different concept of yourself, everything would be different. You are *what you are*, so everything *is as it is*. The events which you observe are determined by the concept you have of yourself. If you change your concept of yourself, the events ahead of you in time are altered, but, thus altered, they *form again a deterministic sequence* starting from the moment of this changed concept. You are a being with powers of intervention, which enable you, by a change of consciousness, to alter the course of observed events—in fact, to *change your future.*

Deny the evidence of the senses, and assume the feeling of the wish fulfilled. Inasmuch as your assumption is *creative* and forms an atmosphere, your assumption, if it be a noble one, increases your assurance and helps you to reach a higher level of being. If, on the other hand, your assumption be an unlovely one, it hinders you and makes your downward way swifter. Just as the lovely assumptions create a harmonious atmosphere, so the hard and bitter feelings create a hard and bitter atmosphere.

Make your assumptions the highest, noblest, happiest concepts. There is no better time to start than *now.* The present moment is always the most opportune in which to eliminate all unlovely assumptions and to concentrate only on the good.

If you would change your life, you must begin at the very source *with your own basic concept of self.* Outer change, becoming part of organizations, political bodies, religious bodies, is not enough. The cause goes deeper. The essential change must take place *in yourself,* in your own concept of self. You must assume that you are what you want to be and continue therein, for the *reality of your assumption has its being in complete independence of objective fact,* and will clothe itself in flesh if you persist in the feeling of the wish fulfilled. When you know that assumptions, if persisted in, harden into facts, then events which seem to the uninitiated mere accidents will be understood by you to be the logical and inevitable *effects* of your assumption.

The important thing to bear in mind is that you have *infinite free will in choosing your assumptions*, but no power to determine conditions and events. *You can create nothing, but your assumption determines what portion of creation you will experience.*

14. Failure

This book would not be complete without some discussion of *failure* in the attempted use of the law of assumption. It is entirely possible that you either have had or will have a number of failures in this respect—many of them in really important matters. If, having read this book, having a thorough knowledge of the application and working of the law of assumption, you faithfully apply it in an effort to attain some intense desire and fail, what is the reason? If to the question, did you persist enough?, you can answer yes—and still the attainment of your desire was not realized, what is the reason for failure?

The answer to this is the most important factor in the successful use of the law of assumption. *The time it takes your assumption to become fact, your desire to be fulfilled, is directly proportionate to the naturalness of your feeling of already being what you want to be—of already having what you desire.*

The fact that it does not feel *natural* to you to be what you imagine yourself to be is *the secret of your failure.* Regardless of your desire, regardless of how faithfully and intelligently you follow the law if you do not feel *natural* about what you want to be *you will not be it.* If it does not feel natural to you to get a better job you will not get a better job. The whole principle is vividly expressed by the Bible phrase "you die in your sins"—you do not transcend from your present level to the state desired.

How can this feeling of naturalness be achieved? The secret lies in one word *imagination.* For example, this is a very simple illustration. Assume that you are securely chained to a large heavy iron bench. You could not possibly run, in fact you could not even walk. In these circumstances it would not be natural for you to run. You could not even *feel* that it was natural for you to run. But you could easily *imagine* yourself running. In that instant, while your consciousness is filled with your *imagined* running, you have forgotten that you are bound. In *imagination* your running was completely natural.

The essential feeling of naturalness can be achieved by *persistently filling your consciousness with imagination*—imagining yourself being what you want to be or having what you desire.

Progress can spring only from your imagination, from your desire to transcend your present level. What you truly and literally *must* feel is that *with your imagination, all things are possible.* You must realize that changes are not caused by caprice, but by a change of consciousness. You may fail to achieve or sustain the particular state of consciousness necessary to produce the effect you desire. But, once you know that consciousness is the only reality and is the sole creator of your particular world and have burnt this truth into your whole being, then you know that success or failure is entirely in your own hands. Whether or not you are disciplined enough to sustain the required state of consciousness in specific instances has no bearing on the truth of the law itself—that an assumption, if persisted in, will harden into fact. The certainty of the truth of this law must remain despite great disappointment and tragedy—even when you "see the light of life go out and all the world go on as though it were still day." You must not believe that because your assumption failed to materialize, the truth that assumptions do materialize is a lie. If your assumptions are not fulfilled it is because of some error or weakness in your consciousness. However, these errors and weaknesses *can be overcome.* Therefore, press on to the attainment of ever-higher levels by feeling that you *already are* the person you want to be. And remember that the time it takes your assumption to become reality is *proportionate to the naturalness of being it.*

15. Destiny

Your destiny is that which you must inevitably experience. Really it is an infinite number of individual destinies, each of which when attained is the starting place for a new destiny.

Since life is *infinite* the concept of an ultimate destiny is inconceivable. When we understand that consciousness is the only reality, we know that it is the only creator. This means that your consciousness is the creator of your destiny. The fact is, you are creating your destiny every moment, *whether you know it or not*. Much that is good and even wonderful has come into your life without you having any inkling that you were the creator of it.

However, the understanding of the causes of your experience, and the *knowledge that you are the sole creator of the contents of your life, both good and bad, not only make you a much keener observer of all phenomena but through the awareness of the power of your own consciousness, intensifies your appreciation of the richness and grandeur of life.*

Regardless of occasional experiences to the contrary it is *your destiny to rise to higher and higher states of consciousness, and to bring into manifestation more and more of creation's infinite wonders.* Actually you are destined to reach the point where you realize that through your own desire you can consciously create your successive destinies.

The study of this book, with its detailed exposition of consciousness and the operation of the law of assumption, is the master key to the conscious attainment of your highest destiny.

This very day start your new life. Approach every experience in a new frame of mind—with a new state of consciousness. Assume the noblest and the best for yourself in every respect and continue therein.

Make believe—great wonders are possible.

About the Author

NEVILLE GODDARD was one of the most remarkable mystical thinkers of the past century. In more than ten books and thousands of lectures, Neville, the solitary public name that he used, expanded on one radical principle: *the human imagination is God*. As such, he taught, everything that you experience results from your thoughts and feeling states. Born to an Anglican family in Barbados in 1905, Neville travelled to New York City at age seventeen in the early 1920s to study theater. Although he won roles on Broadway and toured internationally with a dance troupe, Neville abandoned the stage in the early 1930s to dedicate himself to metaphysical studies and chart a new career as a writer and lecturer. He was a compelling presence at metaphysical churches, spiritual centers, and auditoriums until his death in West Hollywood, California, in 1972. Neville was not widely known during his lifetime, but today his books and lectures, which he permitted to be freely recorded and are now circulated online, have attained bounding popularity. Neville's principles about the creative properties of the mind prefigured some of today's most radical quantum theorizing, and have influenced several major spiritual writers, including Carlos Castaneda and Joseph Murphy.

The Power of Concentration

THE POWER OF CONCENTRATION

The Classic to Harnessing Your Mental Power

From the Immortal Author of *The Kybalion*

by Theron Q. Dumont

Contents

INTRODUCTION
The Voice of a Pioneer *by Mitch Horowitz*   119

FOREWORD   122

LESSON I
Concentration Finds the Way   124

LESSON II
The Self-Mastery Power of Concentration   127

LESSON III
**How to Gain What You Want
Through Concentration**   134

LESSON IV
The Silent Force that Produces Results   137

LESSON V
How Concentrated Thought Links All Humanity 139

LESSON VI
The Training of the Will to Do 142

LESSON VII
The Concentrated Mental Demand 146

LESSON VIII
Concentrating Gives Mental Poise 149

LESSON IX
Concentration Can Overcome Bad Habits 154

LESSON X
Business Results Gained Through Concentration 158

LESSON XI
Concentrate on Your Courage 162

LESSON XII
Concentrate on Wealth 166

LESSON XIII
You Can Concentrate, But Will You? 170

LESSON XIV
**The Art of Concentration
with Practical Exercises** 173

LESSON XV
Concentrate So You Will Not Forget 178

LESSON XVI
**How Concentration
Can Fulfill Your Desire** 180

LESSON XVII
Ideals Develop by Concentration 184

LESSON XVIII
Concentration Reviewed 186

ABOUT THE AUTHOR 190

Introduction

The Voice of a Pioneer
by Mitch Horowitz

If you're an avid reader of metaphysical books, as I am, you might find the voice in this valuable little volume, published in 1916, somewhat familiar.

It belongs to the remarkably energetic New Thought philosopher and publisher William Walker Atkinson, who wrote under several pseudonyms and produced nearly one hundred New Thought books in the three decades leading up to his death in 1932. The most popular of these works was *The Kybalion*, which Atkinson wrote under the name "Three Initiates" in 1908, eight years before this similarly enduring volume.

In *The Power of Concentration,* Atkinson used the name French name of Theron Q. Dumont, which was often his chosen byline to explore matters of psychology, willpower, suggestion, and self-hypnosis, all of which were closely associated with French thinkers in the early twentieth century. This was particularly the case with hypnosis, which was introduced in its earliest form in Paris in the late 1770s by occult healer Franz Anton Mesmer. Although the arrival of the France Revolution, and the ensuing years of social upheaval, interrupted the progress of hypnotic theory in France, the nation once more popularized the therapeutic uses of the craft in the late-nineteenth century through the so-called Nancy School of hypnotism, which promoted practices of suggestion and hypnotherapy. The Nancy movement produced the immensely popular French healer Emile Coué, who became famous in Europe and America in the 1910s and 20s for his self-help mantra, "Day by day, in every way, I am getting better and better."

This was the tradition to which Atkinson sought to attach himself with his persona Theron Q. Dumont. Under the name Dumont, he wrote several works on the power of personal magnetism, the uses of will and suggestion, and the self-shaping forces of the mind, of which *The Power of Concentration* is probably the most compelling, persuasive, and enduring.

As is often the case with Atkinson's works, the book is a feast of practicality and idealism. It is at once inspiring and hard-knuckled—there is no toleration for dreamy visualizations unmoored from outer action. Rather, *The Power of Concentration* shows how to harness your thoughts and habits to heighten your personal performance. Nearly every page contains injunctions to act, do, and strive.

The book's advice, reduced to its essentials in this condensation, remains potent and fresh more than a century after its publication. Atkinson's language often prefigures terms and concepts heard today in the fields of neuroplasticity and cognitive behavioral therapy. Yet his book contains an infectious dynamism and scale of purpose rarely found in either of those fields. The book captures both the epic hopes and the applicability of the early days of New Thought. Its techniques have never been eclipsed or surpassed.

Foreword

We all know that in order to accomplish a certain thing we must concentrate. It is of the utmost value to learn how to concentrate. To make a success of anything, you must be able to concentrate your entire thought upon the idea.

Do not become discouraged if you are unable to hold your thought on the subject very long at first. Very few can. It seems a peculiar fact that it is easier to concentrate on something that is *not* good for us than on something that is beneficial. This tendency is overcome when we learn to concentrate consciously.

Did you ever stop to think what an important part your thoughts play in your life? This book shows their far-reaching and all-abiding effects.

Man is a wonderful creature, but requires training and development to be useful. A great work can be accomplished by every man if he can be awakened to do his very best. But the greatest man would accomplish little if he lacked concentration and effort. Dwarfs can do the work of giants when they are transformed by the almost-magical power of great mental concentration. But giants will only do the work of dwarfs when they lack this power.

We accomplish more by concentration than by fitness; the man that is apparently best suited for a place does not always fill it best. It is the man who concentrates on every possibility that makes an art of both his work, and his life.

This course will stimulate and inspire you to achieve success; it will bring you into perfect harmony with the laws of success. It will give you a firmer hold on your duties and responsibilities.

The methods of thought-concentration given in this work, if put into practice, will open up interior avenues that will connect you with the everlasting laws of Being and their exhaustless foundation of unchangeable truth.

Lesson I
Concentration Finds the Way

Everyone has two natures. One wants to advance and the other wants to pull back. The one that we cultivate and concentrate on decides what we are at the end. Both natures are vying for control. The will alone decides the issue. A man by one supreme effort of the will may change his whole career, and almost accomplish miracles. You may be that man. You can be if you Will to be, for Will can find a way, or make one.

It is a matter of choice whether we allow our diviner self to control us, or whether we get controlled by the brute within. No man has to do anything he does not want to do. He is therefore the director of his life, if he wills to be. What we do is the result of our training. We are like putty, and can be completely controlled by our willpower.

Many people read good books, but say they do not get much out of them. They do not realize that all any book or lesson can do is to awaken them to their possibilities. One of the most beneficial practices I know of is looking for the good in everyone and everything, for there is good in all things. We encourage a person by seeing his good qualities, and we also help ourselves by looking for them. We gain their good wishes, a most valuable asset. We get back what we give out. The time comes when most all of us need encouragement; need buoying up. So, form the habit of encouraging others, and you will find it a wonderful tonic for both others and yourself, for you will get back encouraging and uplifting thoughts.

The first of each month, a person should sit down and examine the progress he has made. If he has not come up to expectations he should discover the reason, and by extra exertion measure up to what is demanded.

I know that every man who is willing to pay the price can be a success. The price is not in money, but in effort. The first essential quality for success is the desire to do—*to be something*. The next thing is to learn how to do it; the next to carry it into execution. The man best able to accomplish anything is the one with a broad mind; a man may acquire knowledge that is foreign to a particular case, but is, nevertheless, of some value in all cases. So, the man who wants to be successful must be liberal; he must acquire all the knowledge he can; he must be well posted not only in one branch of his business but in every part of it. Such a man achieves success.

The secret of success is to try always to improve yourself no matter where you are or what your position. Learn all you can. Don't see how little you can do, but how much you can do. Such a man will always be in demand.

The man with grit and will may be poor today and wealthy in a few years; willpower is a better asset than money. Will will carry you over chasms of failure, if you but give it the chance.

Everyone *really wants* to do something, but few will put forward the effort to make the necessary sacrifice to secure it. There is only one way to accomplish anything, and that is to go ahead and do it. A man may accomplish almost anything today, if he just sets his heart on it and lets nothing interfere with his progress. Obstacles are quickly overcome by the man that sets out to accomplish his heart's desire. The "bigger" the man, the smaller the obstacle appears. The "smaller" the man the greater the obstacle appears. Always look at the advantage you gain by overcoming obstacles, and it will give you the needed courage for their conquest.

Lesson II

The Self-Mastery Power of Concentration

Man from a psychological standpoint of development is not what he should be. He does not possess the self-mastery, the self-directing power of concentration that is his right.

He has not trained himself to promote his self-mastery. Every balanced mind possesses faculties whose chief duties are to engineer, direct, and concentrate the operations of the mind, both in a mental and physical sense. Man must learn to control not only his mind but also his bodily movements.

When the self-regulating faculties are not developed the impulses, appetites, emotions, and passions have full swing, and the mind becomes impulsive, restless, emotional, and irregular. This makes mental concentration poor.

When the self-guiding faculties are weak, the person always lacks the power of mental concentration. Therefore, you cannot concentrate until you develop those very powers that *qualify* you to concentrate. If you cannot concentrate, one of the following is the cause:

1. Deficiency of the motor centers.
2. An impulsive and emotional mind.
3. An untrained mind.

The last fault can soon be removed by systematic practice. It is easiest to correct.

The impulsive and emotional state of mind can best be corrected by restraining anger, passion and excitement, hatred, strong impulses, intense emotions, fretfulness, etc. It is impossible to concentrate when you are in any of these excited states. You can help naturally decrease these by avoiding food and drinks as have nerve weakening or stimulating influences, or a tendency to stir up the passions, impulses, and emotions. It is also a good practice to watch and associate with people who are steady, calm, controlled, and conservative.

Many have the idea that when they get into a negative state they are concentrating, but this is not so. Their power of concentration becomes weaker, and they find it difficult to concentrate on anything. The mind that cannot center itself on a special subject or thought, is weak; as is the mind that cannot draw itself from a subject or thought. But the person who can center his mind on any problem, no matter what it is, and remove any unharmonious impressions, has strength of mind. Concentration, first, last, and all the time, means strength of mind.

A concentrated mind pays attention to thoughts, words, acts, and plans. The person who allows his mind to roam at will, will never accomplish a great deal in the world. He wastes his energies. You concentrate the moment you say, "I want to, I can, I will."

Concentration of the mind can only be developed by watching yourself closely. All kinds of development commence with close attention. You should regulate your every thought and feeling. When you commence to watch yourself, your own acts, and also the acts of other people, you use the faculties of autonomy, and, as you continue to do so, you improve your faculties, until in time you can engineer your every thought, wish, and plan. Only the trained mind can focalize. To hold a thought before it until all the faculties have had time to consider that thought is concentration.

The person who cannot direct his thoughts, wishes, plans, resolutions, and studies cannot possibly succeed to the fullest extent. The person who is impulsive one moment and calm the next has not the proper control over himself. He is not a master of his mind, nor of his thoughts, feelings, and wishes. Such a person cannot be a success. When he becomes irritated, he irritates others and spoils all chances of any concerned doing their best. But the person who can direct his energies and hold them at work in a concentrated manner controls his every work and act, and thereby gains power to control others. He can make his every move serve a useful end, and every thought a noble purpose.

He is consciously attentive and holds his mind to one thing at a time. He shuts out everything else. When you are talking to anyone give him your sole and undivided attention. Do not let your attention wander or be diverted. Give no heed to anything else, but make your will and intellect act in unison.

Start out in the morning and see how self-poised you can remain all day. At times, take an inventory of your actions during the day and see if you have kept your determination. If not, see that you do tomorrow. The more self-poised you are the better your concentration. Never be in too much of a hurry; and, remember, the more you improve your concentration, the greater are your possibilities. Concentration means success, because you are better able to govern yourself and centralize your mind; you become more in earnest in what you do, and this almost invariably improves your chances for success.

When you are talking to a person have your own plans in mind. Concentrate your strength upon the purpose you are talking about. Watch his every move, but keep your own plans before you. Unless you do, you will waste your energy and not accomplish as much as you should.

I want you to watch the next person you see who has the reputation of being a strong character, a man of force. Watch and see what a perfect control he has over his body. Then I want you to watch just an ordinary person. Notice how he moves his eyes, arms, fingers; notice the useless expenditure of energy. These movements lessen the person's power in vital and nerve directions. Center your mind on one purpose, one plan, one transaction.

There is nothing that uses up nerve force so quickly as excitement. This is why an irritable person is never magnetic; he is never admired or loved; he does not develop those finer qualities that a real gentleman possesses. Anger, sarcasm, and excitement weaken a person in this direction. The person that allows himself to get excited will become nervous in time, because he uses up his nerve forces and his vital energies. The person that cannot control himself and keep from becoming excited cannot concentrate.

But those whose actions are slower and directed by their intelligence develop concentration. Sometimes dogmatic, willful, excitable persons can concentrate, but it is spasmodic, erratic concentration instead of controlled and uniform concentration. Their energy works by spells; sometimes they have plenty, other times very little; it is easily excited; easily wasted. The best way to understand it is to compare it with the discharge of a gun. If the gun goes off when you want it to, it accomplishes the purpose, but if it goes off before you are ready, you not only waste ammunition, but are also likely to do some damage. That is just what most people do. They allow their energy to explode, thus not only wasting it, but also endangering others. They waste their power, their magnetism, and so injure their chance of success.

The brain is the storehouse of the energy. Most all persons have all the dynamic energy they need if they would concentrate it. They have the machine, but they must also have the engineer, or they will not go very far. The engineer is the self-regulating, directing power. The good engineer controls his every act. By what you do you either advance or degenerate. This is a good idea to keep always in mind. When you are uncertain whether you should do something, just think whether by doing it you will grow or deteriorate, and act accordingly.

I am a firm believer in "work when you work, play when you play." When you give yourself up to pleasure you can develop concentration by thinking of nothing else but pleasure; when your mind dwells on love, think of nothing but this and you will find you can develop a more intense love than you ever had before. When you concentrate your mind on the "you" or real self, and its wonderful possibilities, you develop concentration and a higher opinion of yourself. By doing this systematically, you develop power, because you cannot be systematic without concentrating on what you are doing. When you walk out into the country and inhale the fresh air, studying vegetation, trees, etc., you are concentrating. Whenever you fix your mind on a certain thought and hold your mind on it at successive intervals, you develop concentration.

If you hold your mind on some chosen object, you centralize your attention, just like the lens of the camera centralizes on a certain landscape. Therefore, always hold your mind on what you are doing, no matter what it is.

Practice inhaling long, deep breaths, not simply for the improvement of health, although that is no small matter, but also for the purpose of developing more power, more love, more life. All work assists in development.

If you want to get more out of life you must think more of love. Unless you have real affection for something, you have no sentiment, no sweetness, no magnetism. So arouse your love affections by your will, and enter into a fuller life.

The next time you feel yourself becoming irritable, use your will and be patient. This is a very good exercise in self-control. It will help you to keep patient if you will breathe slowly and deeply. If you find you are commencing to speak fast, just control yourself and speak slowly and clearly. Keep from either raising or lowering your voice, and concentrate on the fact that you are determined to keep your poise, and you will improve your power of concentration.

If you feel yourself getting irritable, nervous or weak, stand squarely on your feet with your chest up and inhale deeply, and you will see that your irritability will disappear and a silent calm will pass over you.

If you are in the habit of associating with nervous, irritable people, quit it until you grow strong in the power of concentration, because irritable, angry, fretful, dogmatic, and disagreeable people will weaken what powers of resistance you have.

When your eye is steady, your mind is steady. One of the best ways to study a person is to watch his physical movements, for, when we study his actions, we are studying his mind. Because actions are the expressions of the mind. As the mind is, so is the action. When you learn to control the body, you are gaining control over the mind.

Lesson III

How to Gain What You Want Through Concentration

The ignorant person may say, "How can you get anything by merely wanting it?" I say that through concentration you can get anything you want. Every desire can be gratified. But whether it is, will depend upon you concentrating to have that desire fulfilled. Merely wishing for something will not bring it. Wishing you had something shows a weakness, and not a belief that you will really get it. So never merely wish, as we are not living in a "fairy age." You use up just as much brain force in "vain imaginings" as you do when you think of something worthwhile.

Be careful of your desires, make a mental picture of what you want and set your will to this until it materializes. Never allow yourself to drift without helm or rudder. Know what you want to do, and strive with all your might to do it, and you will succeed.

Feel that you can accomplish anything you undertake. Many undertake to do things, but feel when they start they are going to fail, and usually they do. I will give an illustration. A man goes to a store for an article. The clerk says, "I am sorry, we do not have it." But the man that is determined to get that thing inquires if he doesn't know where he can get it. Again receiving an unsatisfactory answer the determined buyer consults the manager, and finally finds where the article can be bought.

That is the whole secret of concentrating on getting what you want. And, remember, your soul is a center of all-power, and you can accomplish what you will to. "I'll find a way or make one!" is the spirit that wins. I know a man who is now head of a large bank. He started there as a messenger boy. His father had a button made for him with a "P" on it and put it on his coat. He said, "Son, that 'P' is a reminder that some day you are to be the president of your bank. I want you to keep this thought in your mind. Every day do something that will put you nearer your goal." Each night after supper he would say, "Son, what did you do today?" In this way the thought was always kept in mind. He concentrated on becoming president of that bank, and he did. His father told him never to tell anyone what that "P" stood for. His associates made a good deal of fun of it. And they tried to find out what it stood for, but they never did until he was made president, and then he told the secret.

Don't waste your mental powers in wishes. Don't dissipate your energies by trying to satisfy every whim. Concentrate on doing something really worthwhile. The man that sticks to something is not the man that fails.

> *"Power to him who power exerts."*
> —EMERSON

This great universe is interwoven with myriad forces. You make your own place, and whether it is important depends upon you. Through the Indestructible and Unconquerable Law you can, in time, accomplish all right things, and therefore do not be afraid to undertake whatever you really desire to accomplish and are willing to pay for in effort. *Anything that is right is possible.* That which is necessary will inevitably take place. If something is right, it is your duty to do it, though the whole world thinks it to be wrong.

"God and one are always a majority," or in plain words, that omnipotent interior law which is God, and the organism that represents you, is able to conquer the whole world if your cause is absolutely just. Don't say, "I wish I were great." You can do anything that is proper, and that you want to. Just say: You can. You will. You must. *Realize this* and the rest is easy.

Lesson IV

The Silent Force That Produces Results

Through concentrated thought power you can make yourself whatever you please. By thought you can greatly increase your efficiency and strength. You are surrounded by all kinds of thoughts, some good, others bad, and you are sure to absorb some of the latter if you do not build up a positive mental attitude.

If you will study the needless moods of anxiety, worry, despondency, discouragement, and others that are the result of uncontrolled thoughts, you will realize how important the control of your thoughts are. Your thoughts make you what you are.

When I walk along the street and study the different people's faces I can tell how they spent their lives. It all shows in their faces, just like a mirror reflects their physical countenances. In looking in those faces I cannot help thinking how most of the people you see have wasted their lives.

Understanding the power of thought will awaken possibilities within you that you never dreamed of. Never forget that your thoughts are making your environment and your friends, and as your thoughts change these will also.

The desire to do right carries with it a great power. I want you to thoroughly realize the importance of your thoughts, and how to make them valuable, to understand that your thoughts come to you over invisible wires and influence you.

In order to speak wisely you must secure at least a partial concentration of the faculties and forces upon the subject at hand. Speech interferes with the focusing powers of the mind, as it withdraws the attention to the external and therefore is hardly to be compared with that deep silence of the subconscious mind, where deep thoughts, and the silent forces of high potency, are evolved. It is necessary to be silent before you can speak wisely. The person who is really alert, well poised, and able to speak wisely under trying circumstances, is the person who has practiced in the silence. Most people do not know what the silence is and think it is easy to go into the silence, but this is not so. In the real silence, we become attached to that interior law and the forces become silent, because they are in a state of high potency. Hold the thought: *In silence I will allow my higher self to-have-complete-control. I-will-be-true-to-my-higher-self. I will live true to my conception of what is right. I realize that it is in my self-interest to live up to my best. I demand wisdom so that I may act wisely for myself and others.*

In the next chapter, I tell you of the mysterious law that links all humanity together by the powers of cooperative thought, and chooses for us companionship and friends.

Lesson V

How Concentrated Thought Links All Humanity

Success is the result of how you think. I will show you how to think to be successful.

The power to rule and attract success is within yourself. The barriers that shut these off from you are subject to your control. You have unlimited power to think, and this is the link that connects you with your omniscient source.

Success is the result of certain moods of mind or ways of thinking. These moods can be controlled by you, and produced at will.

Concentrated thought will accomplish seemingly impossible results and make you realize your fondest ambitions. At the same time that you break down barriers of limitation new ambitions will be awakened. If you will just realize that through deep concentration you become linked with thoughts of omnipotence, you will kill out entirely your belief in your limitations, and at the same time will drive away all fear and other negative and destructive thought forces, which constantly work against you.

It is just as easy to surround your life with what you want as it is with what you don't. It is a question to be decided by your will. There are no walls to prevent you from getting what you want, *providing you want what is right*. If you choose something that is not right, you are in opposition to the omnipotent plans of the universe, and deserve to fail. *But, if you base your desires on justice and good will, you avail yourself of the helpful powers of universal currents, and instead of having a handicap to work against, can depend upon ultimate success, though the outward appearances may not at first be bright.*

Never stop to think of temporary appearances, but maintain an unfaltering belief in your ultimate success. Make your plans carefully, and see that they are not contrary to the tides of universal justice. The main thing for you to remember is to keep at bay the destructive and opposing forces of fear, anger, and their satellites.

There is no power so great as the belief which comes from the knowledge that your thought is in harmony with the divine laws of thought, and the sincere conviction that your cause is right.

All just causes succeed in time, though temporarily they may fail. So if you should face the time when everything seems against you, quiet your fears, drive away all destructive thoughts, and uphold the dignity of your moral and spiritual life.

The following method may assist you in gaining better thought control. If you are unable to control your fears, just say to your faulty determination, "Do not falter or be afraid, for I am not really alone. I am surrounded by invisible forces that will assist me to remove the unfavorable appearances." Soon you will have more courage. The only difference between the fearless man and the fearful one is in his will, his hope. So if you lack success, believe in it, hope for it, claim it. You can use the same method to brace up your thoughts of desire, aspiration, imagination, expectation, ambition, understanding, trust, and assurance.

If you get anxious, angry, discouraged, undecided or worried, it is because you are not receiving the cooperation of the higher powers of your mind. By your Will you can so organize the powers of the mind that your moods change only as you want them to instead of as circumstances affect you. If you allow the mind to wander while you are doing small things, it will be likely to get into mischief and make it hard to concentrate on the important act when it comes.

The will does not act with clearness, decision and promptness *unless it is trained to do so.* Comparatively few people really know what they are doing every minute of the day. This is because they do not observe with sufficient orderliness and accuracy. It is not difficult to know what you are doing all the time, if you will just practice concentration, and with a reposeful deliberation train yourself to think clearly, promptly, and decisively.

If you allow yourself to worry or hurry in what you are doing, it will not be clearly photographed upon the sensitized plate of the subjective mind, and therefore you will not be really conscious of your actions. So practice accuracy and concentration of thought, and also absolute truthfulness, and you will soon be able to concentrate.

Lesson VI
The Training of the Will to Do

The Will To Do is the greatest power in the world that is concerned with human accomplishment, and no one can predetermine its limits.

The Will To Do is a force that is strictly practical, yet it is difficult to explain just what it is. It can be compared to electricity because we know it only through its cause and effects. Every time you accomplish any definite act, consciously or unconsciously, you use the principle of the Will. You can Will to do anything, whether right or wrong, and therefore how you use your will makes a big difference in your life.

Every person possesses some "Will To Do." It is the inner energy that controls all conscious acts. *Genius is but a will to do little things with infinite pains. Little things done well open the door of opportunity for bigger things.*

Study yourself carefully. Find out your greatest weakness and then use your willpower to overcome it. In this way eradicate your faults, one by one, until you have built up a strong character and personality.

Rules for Improvement. A desire arises. Now think whether this would be good for you. If it is not, use your Willpower to kill out the desire; but, on the other hand, if it is a righteous desire, summon all your Willpower to your aid, crush all obstacles that confront you, and secure possession of the coveted Good.

Slowness in Making Decisions. This is a weakness of Willpower. You know you should do something, but you delay doing it through lack of decision. It is easier not to do a certain thing , but conscience says to do it. The vast majority of people are failures because of the lack of deciding to do a thing when it should be done. Those that are successful have been quick to grasp opportunities by making a quick decision. This power of will can be used to bring culture, wealth, and health.

Some Special Pointers. For the next week try to make quicker decisions in your little daily affairs. Set the hour you wish to get up and arise exactly at the fixed time. Anything that you should accomplish, do on or ahead of time. You want, of course, to give due deliberation to weighty matters, but by making quick decisions on little things you will acquire the ability to make quick decisions in bigger things.

You Are as Good as Anyone. You have willpower, and if you use it, you will get your share of the luxuries of life. So use it to claim your own. Don't depend on anyone else to help you. We have to fight our own battles. All the world loves a fighter, while the coward is despised by all. Every person's problems are different, so I can only say "analyze your opportunities and conditions and study your natural abilities." Don't make an indefinite plan, but a definite one, and then don't give up until your object has been accomplished. Put these suggestions into practice with true earnestness, and you will soon note astonishing results, and your whole life will be completely changed. An excellent motto for one of pure motives is: *Through my willpower I dare do what I want to.* You will find this affirmation has a very strengthening effect.

The Spirit of Perseverance. The spirit of "sticktoitiveness" is the one that wins. Many go just so far and then give up, whereas, if they had persevered a little longer, they would have won out. Many have much initiative, but instead of concentrating it into one channel they diffuse it through several, thereby dissipating it to such an extent that its effect is lost.

Lack of Perseverance is nothing but the lack of the Will To Do. It takes the same energy to say, "I will continue," as to say, "I give up." Just the moment you say the latter you shut off your dynamo, and your determination is gone. Every time you allow your determination to be broken you weaken it. Don't forget this. Just the instant you notice your determination beginning to weaken, concentrate on it and by sheer Will Power make it continue on the "job."

Never try to make a decision when you are not in a calm state of mind. If in a "quick temper," you are likely to say things you regret. In anger, you follow impulse rather than reason. No one can expect to achieve success if he makes decisions when not in full control of his mental forces. Therefore make it a fixed rule to make decisions only when at your best.

Special Instructions to Develop the Will To Do. This is a form of mental energy, but requires the proper mental attitude to make it manifest. We hear of people having wonderful willpower, which really is wrong. It should be said that they *use* their willpower, while with many it is a latent force. I want you to realize that no one has a monopoly on willpower. What we speak of as willpower is but the gathering together of mental energy, the concentration of power at one point. So never think of someone as having a stronger will than you. Each person will be supplied with just that amount of willpower that he demands.

Lesson VII

The Concentrated Mental Demand

The Mental Demand is the potent force in achievement. The attitude of the mind affects the expression of the face, determines action, changes our physical condition, and regulates our lives.

The mental demand must be directed by every power of the mind, and every possible element should be used to make the demand materialize. You can so intently desire a thing that you can exclude all distracting thoughts. When you practice this singleness of concentration until you attain the end sought, you have developed a Will capable of accomplishing whatever you wish.

The men looked upon as the world's successes have not always been men of great physical power, nor at the start did they seem very well adapted to the conditions around them. In the beginning, they were not considered men of superior genius, but they won their success by their resolution to achieve results by permitting no setback to dishearten them; no difficulties to daunt them. Nothing could turn them or influence them against their determination. They never lost sight of their goal. In all of us there is this silent force of wonderful power. If developed, it can overcome conditions that would seem insurmountable.

It is constantly urging us on to greater achievement. The more we become acquainted with it the better strategists we become, the more courage we develop, and the greater the desire within us for self-expression along many lines.

No one will ever be a failure if he becomes conscious of this silent force within that controls his destiny. But without the consciousness of this inner force, you will not have a clear vision, and external conditions will not yield to the power of your mind. It is the mental resolve that makes achievement possible. Once this has been formed it should never be allowed to cease to press its claim until its object is attained.

Perseverance is the first element of success. In order to persevere you must be ceaseless in your application. It requires you to concentrate your thoughts upon your undertaking, and bring every energy to bear upon keeping them focused upon it until you have accomplished your aim. To quit short of this is to weaken all future efforts.

The Mental Demand seems an unreal power because it is intangible; but it is the mightiest power in the world. It is a power that is free for you to use. No one can use it for you. Every time you make a Mental Demand you strengthen the brain centers by drawing to you external forces.

Few realize the power of a Mental Demand. It is possible to make your demand so strong that you can impart what you have to say to another without speaking to him. Have you ever, after planning to discuss a certain matter with a friend, had the experience of having him broach the subject before you had a chance to speak of it? These things are neither coincidences nor accidents, but are the results of mental demand launched by strong concentration. The person that never wants anything gets little. To demand resolutely is the first step toward getting what you want.

Once the Mental Demand is made, however, never let it falter. If you do, the current that connects you with your desire is broken. Take all the necessary time to build a firm foundation, so that there need not be even an element of doubt to creep in. Just the moment you entertain "doubt" you lose some of the demand force, and force once lost is hard to regain. So whenever you make a mental demand hold steadfastly to it until your need is supplied.

And every man of AVERAGE ability, the ordinary man that you see about you, can be really successful, independent, free of worry, HIS OWN MASTER, if he can manage to do just two things: First, remain forever dissatisfied with what he IS doing and with what he HAS accomplished. Second, develop in his mind a belief that the word "impossible" was not intended for him. Build up in his mind the confidence that enables the mind to use its power.

Lesson VIII
Concentration Gives Mental Poise

You will find that the man that concentrates is well poised, whereas the man that allows his mind to wander is easily upset. When in this state wisdom does not pass from the subconscious storehouse into the consciousness. There must be mental quiet before the two forms of consciousness can work in harmony. When you are able to concentrate, you have peace of mind.

If you are in the habit of losing your poise, form the habit of reading literature that has a quieting power. Just the second you feel your poise slipping, say, "Peace," and then hold this thought in mind and you will never lose your self-control. Think of yourself as a child of the infinite, possessing infinite possibilities. Write on a piece of paper, "I have the power to do and to be whatever I wish to do and be." Keep this mentally before you, and you will find the thought will be of great help to you.

The Mistake of Concentrating on Your Business While Away. In order to be successful today, you must concentrate, but don't become a slave to concentration, and carry your business cares home. Just as sure as you do, you will be burning the life forces at both ends, and the fire will go out much sooner than intended.

Many men become so absorbed in their business that when they go to church they do not hear the preacher because their minds are on their business. If they go to the theater they do not enjoy it because their business is on their minds. When they go to bed they think about business instead of sleep. This is the wrong kind of concentration and is dangerous. It is involuntary. It is a big mistake to let a thought rule you, instead of ruling it. He who does not rule himself is not a success. If you cannot control your concentration, your health will suffer.

Never become so absorbed with anything that you cannot lay it aside and take up another. This is self-control. Concentration is paying attention to a chosen thought.

Self-Study Valuable. Everyone has some habits that can be overcome by concentration. We will say for instance, you are in the habit of complaining, or finding fault with yourself or others; or, imagining that you do not possess the ability of others; or feeling that you are not as good as someone else; or that you cannot rely on yourself; or harboring any similar thoughts. These should be cast aside, and instead thoughts of strength should be put in their place. Just remember that every time you think of yourself as being weak, in some way you are making yourself so. Our mental conditions make us what we are. Just watch yourself and see how much time you waste in worrying, fretting, and complaining. The more of it you do, the worse off you are.

Just the minute you are aware of thinking a negative thought immediately change to a positive one. If you start to think of failure, change to thinking of success. You have the germ of success within you. Care for it the same as the setting hen broods over the eggs, and you can make it a reality.

You can make those that you come in contact with feel as you do, because you radiate vibrations of the way you feel, and your vibrations are felt by others. When you concentrate on a certain thing you turn all the rays of your vibrations on this. Thought is the directing power of all Life's vibrations. If a person should enter a room with a lot of people and feel as if he were a person of no consequence, no one would know he was there unless they saw him; and even if they did, they would not remember seeing him, because they were not attracted towards him. But let him enter the room feeling that he was magnetic and concentrating on this thought, others would feel his vibration. So remember, the way you feel you can make others feel.

If you will study all of the great characters of history you will find that they were enthusiastic. First, they were enthusiastic themselves, and then they could arouse others' enthusiasm. It is latent in everyone. It is a wonderful force when once aroused. This is the keynote of success.

"Think, speak, and act just as you wish to be, And you will be that which you wish to be."

You are just what you think you are, and not what you may appear to be. You may fool others, but not yourself. You may control your life and actions just as you can control your hands. If you want to raise your hand, you must first think of raising it. If you want to control your life, you must first control your thinking. Easy to do, is it not? Yes it is, if you will but concentrate on what you think about.

How can we secure concentration? To this question, the first and last answer must be: by interest and strong motive. The stronger the motive, the greater the concentration.

Successful Lives Are the Concentrated Lives. Train yourself so that you will be able to centralize your thought, develop your brainpower, and increase your mental energy, or you can be a slacker, a drifter, a quitter, or a sleeper. It all depends on how you concentrate, or centralize your thoughts. Your thinking then becomes a fixed power and you do not waste time thinking about something that would not be good for you. You pick out the thoughts that will be the means of bringing you what you desire, and they become a material reality. Whatever we create in the thought world will some day materialize. That is the law. Never forget this.

Why People Often Do Not Get What They Concentrate On. Because they sit down in hopeless despair and expect it to come to them. But if they will just reach out for it with their biggest effort they will find it is within their reach. No one limits us but ourselves.

Through our concentration we can attract what we want, because we became en rapport with the Universal forces, from which we can get what we want.

A man starts to think on a certain subject. He has all kinds of thoughts come to him, but by concentration he shuts out all these but the one he has chosen. Concentration is just a case of willing to do a certain thing, and doing it.

If you want to accomplish anything, first put yourself in a concentrating, reposeful, receptive, acquiring frame of mind. In tackling unfamiliar work make haste slowly and deliberately, and then you will secure that interior activity, which is never possible when you are in a hurry or under a strain. When you "think hard," or try to hurry results too quickly, you generally shut off the interior flow of thoughts and ideas. You have often no doubt tried hard to think of something but could not, but just as soon as you stopped trying to think of it, it came to you.

Lesson IX

Concentration Can Overcome Bad Habits

Habits make or break us to a far greater extent than we like to admit. Habit is both a powerful enemy and wonderful ally of concentration. You must learn to overcome habits that are injurious to concentration, and to cultivate those that increase it.

Most people are controlled by their habits, and are buffeted around by them like waves of the ocean tossing a piece of wood. They do things in a certain way because of the power of habit. They seldom ever think of concentrating on why they do them this or that way, or study to see if they could do them in a better way.

The first thing I want you to realize is that all habits are governed consciously or unconsciously by the will. Most of us are forming new habits all the time. Very often, if you repeat something several times in the same way, you will have formed the habit of doing it that way. But the oftener you repeat it the stronger that habit grows, and the more deeply it becomes embedded in your nature. After a habit has been in force for a long time, it becomes almost a part of you, and is therefore hard to overcome. But you can still break any habit by strong concentration on its opposite.

You will find the following maxims worth remembering.

First Maxim: "We must make our nervous system our ally instead of our enemy."

Second Maxim: "In the acquisition of a new habit as in the leaving off of an old one, we must take care to launch ourselves with as strong and decided an initiative as possible."

Surround yourself with every aid you can. Don't play with fire by forming bad habits. Make a new beginning today. Study why you have been doing certain things. If they are not for your good, shun them henceforth. Don't give in to a single temptation, for every time you do, you strengthen the chain of bad habits. Every time you keep a resolution you break the chain that enslaves you.

Third Maxim: "Never allow an exception to occur till the new habit is securely rooted in your life."

Fourth Maxim: "Seize the very first possible opportunity to act on every resolution you make, and on every emotional prompting you may experience in the direction of the habits you aspire to gain."

Keep every resolution you make, for you not only profit by the resolution, but it furnishes you with an exercise that causes the brain cells and physiological correlatives to form the habit of adjusting themselves to carry out resolutions. A tendency to act becomes effectively engrained in us in proportion to the uninterrupted frequency with which the actions actually occur, and the brain "grows" to their use.

Fifth Maxim: "Keep the faculty of effort alive in you by a little gratuitous exercise every day."

The more we exercise the will, the better we can control our habits. Every few days, do something for no other reason than its difficulty, so that when the hour of dire need draws near, it may find you not unnerved or untrained to stand the test. Asceticism of this sort is like the insurance that a man pays on his house and goods. So with the man who has daily insured himself to habits of concentrated attention, energetic volition, and self-denial in unnecessary things.

Habits have often been called a labor-saving invention, because when they are formed they require less of both mental and material strength. The more deeply the habit becomes ingrained, the more automatic it becomes. Therefore habit is an economizing tendency of our nature, for if it were not for habit we should have to be more watchful. We walk across a crowded street; the habit of stopping and looking prevents us from being hurt. Habits mean less risk, less fatigue, and greater accuracy.

In order to overcome undesirable habits, two things are necessary. You must have trained your will to do what you want it to do, and the stronger the will the easier it will be to break a habit. Then you must make a resolution to do just the opposite of what the habit is. I will bring this chapter to a close by giving Doctor Oppenheim's instructions for overcoming a habit:

"If you want to abolish a habit, and its accumulated circumstances as well, you must grapple with the matter as earnestly as you would with a physical enemy. You must go into the encounter with all tenacity of determination, with all fierceness of resolve—and yea, even with a passion for success that may be called vindictive. No human enemy can be as insidious, so persevering, as unrelenting as an unfavorable habit. It never sleeps, it needs no rest.

"It is like a parasite that grows with the growth of the supporting body, and, like a parasite, it can best be killed by violent separation and crushing."

It is not in the easy, contented moments of our life that we make our greatest progress, for then it requires no special effort to keep in tune. But it is when we are in the midst of trials and misfortunes, when we think we are sinking, being overwhelmed, then it is important for us to realize that we are linked to a great Power, and if we live as we should, there is nothing that can occur in life that could permanently injure us, nothing can happen that should disturb us. Always remember you have within you unlimited power, ready to manifest itself in the form which fills our need at the moment.

Lesson X

Business Results Through Concentration

Business success depends on well-concentrated efforts. You must use every mental force you can master. The more these are used, the more they increase. Therefore the more you accomplish today the more force you will have at your disposal to solve your problems tomorrow. Then when you have resolved what you want to do, you will be drawn towards it. There is a law that opens the way to the fulfillment of your desires. Of course, back of your desire you must put forward the necessary effort to carry out your purpose; you must use your power to put your desires into force. Once they are created, and you keep up your determination to have them fulfilled, you both consciously and unconsciously work toward their materialization. Set your heart on your purpose, concentrate your thought upon it, direct your efforts with all your intelligence, and in due time you will realize your ambition.

Feel yourself a success, believe you are a success, and thus put yourself in the attitude that demands recognition and the thought current draws to you what you need to make you a success. Don't be afraid of big undertakings.

Go at them with grit, and pursue methods that you think will accomplish your purpose. You may not at first meet with entire success, but aim so high that if you fall a little short you will still have accomplished much.

What others have done you can do. You may even do what others have been unable to do. Always keep a strong desire to succeed in your mind. Be in love with your aim and work, and make it, as far as possible, square with the rule of the greatest good to the greatest number, and your life cannot be a failure.

The successful business attitude must be cultivated to make the most out of your life: the attitude of expecting great things from both yourself and others. This alone will often cause men to make good; to measure up to the best that is in them.

It is not the spasmodic spurts that count on a long journey, but the steady efforts. Spurts fatigue, and make it hard for you to continue.

When once you reach a conclusion abide by it. Let there be no doubt, or wavering. If you are uncertain about every decision you make, you will be subject to harassing doubts and fears, which will render your judgment of little value. The man that decides according to what he thinks right, and who learns from every mistake, acquires a well-balanced mind that gets the best results. He gains the confidence of others. He is known as the man who knows what he wants, and not as one that is as changeable as the weather. Reliable firms want to do business with men of known qualities, with men of firmness, judgment, and reliability.

So, if you wish to start in business for yourself, your greatest asset, with the single exception of a sound physique, is that of a good reputation.

A successful business is not hard to build if we can concentrate all our mental forces upon it. We hear people say that business is trying on the nerves, but it is the unsettling elements of fret, worry, and suspense that are nerve exhausting, and not the business. Executing one's plans may cause fatigue, but enjoyment comes with rest. If there has not been any unnatural strain, the recuperative powers replace what energy has been lost.

By attending to each day's work properly, you develop the capacity to do a greater work tomorrow. It is this gradual development that makes possible the carrying out of big plans.

Even brilliant men's conceptions of the possibilities of their mental forces are so limited and below their real worth that they are far more likely to belittle their possibilities than they are to exaggerate them. You don't want to think that an aim is impossible because it has never been realized in the past. Everyday someone is doing something that was never done before.

The natural leader always draws to himself, by the law of mental attraction, all the ideas in his chosen subject that have ever been conceived by others. This is of the greatest importance and help. If you are properly trained you benefit much by others' thoughts, and, providing you generate from within yourself something of value, they will benefit from yours. "We are heirs of all the ages," but we must know how to use our inheritance.

The confident, pushing, hopeful, determined man influences all with whom he associates, and inspires the same qualities in them. There is no reason why your work or business should burn you out. When it does, something is wrong. You are attracting forces and influence that you should not, because you are not in harmony with what you are doing. There is nothing so tiring as trying to do work for which we are unfitted both by temperament and training.

Each one should be engaged in a business that he loves; he should be furthering movements with which he is in sympathy. Only then will he do his best, and take intense pleasure in his business. In this way, while constantly growing and developing his powers, he is at the same time rendering through his work genuine and devoted service to humanity.

Lesson XI

Concentrate On Your Courage

Courage is the backbone of man. The man with courage has persistence. He states what he believes, and puts it into execution.

Lack of courage creates financial, as well as mental and moral difficulties. When a new problem comes, instead of looking upon it as something to be achieved, the man or woman without courage looks for reasons why it cannot be done, and failure is naturally the almost inevitable result. This is a subject well worth your study. Look upon everything within your power as a possibility, and you will accomplish a great deal more, because by considering a thing as impossible you immediately draw to yourself all the elements that contribute to failure. Lack of courage destroys your confidence in yourself.

The man without courage unconsciously draws to himself all that is contemptible, weakening, demoralizing, and destructive. We must first have the courage to *strongly desire something*. A desire to be fulfilled must be backed by the strength of all our mental forces. Such a desire has enough commanding force to change all unfavorable conditions.

What is courage? It is the *Will To Do*. It takes no more energy to be courageous than to be cowardly. It is a matter of the right training, in the right way. Courage concentrates the mental forces on the task at hand. It then directs them thoughtfully, steadily, deliberately, while attracting all the forces of success toward the desired end.

As we are creatures of habits, we should avoid people who lack courage. They are easy to discover because of their habits of fear in attacking new problems. The man with courage is never afraid.

Start out today with the idea that there is no reason why you should not be courageous. If any fear-thoughts come to you, cast them off as you would the deadly viper. Form the habit of never thinking of anything unfavorable to yourself or anyone else. In dealing with difficulties, new or old, hold ever the thought: "I am courageous." Whenever a doubt crosses the threshold of your mind, banish it. Remember, you as master of your mind control its every thought, and here is a good one to often affirm: "I have courage because I desire it; because I need it; because I use it; and because I refuse to become such a weakling as cowardice produces."

There is no justification for the loss of courage. The evils by which you will almost certainly be overwhelmed without it are far greater than those which courage will help you to meet and overcome. Right, then, must be the moralist who says that the only thing to fear is fear.

Never let another's opinion affect you; he cannot tell what you are able to do; he does not know what you can do with your forces. The truth is, you do not know yourself until you put yourself to the test. Therefore, how can someone else know? Never let anyone else put a valuation on you.

Almost all wonderful achievements have been accomplished after it had been "thoroughly" demonstrated that they were impossibilities. Once we understand the law, all things are possible. If they were impossibilities, we could not conceive them.

Just the moment you allow someone to influence you against what you think is right, you lose that confidence that inspires courage and carries with it all the forces that courage creates. Just the moment you begin to swerve in your plan you begin to carry out another's thought, and not your own. You become the directed and not the director. You forsake the courage and resolution of your own mind, and you therefore lack the very forces that you need to sustain and carry out your work. Instead of being self-reliant you become timid, and this invites failure. When you permit yourself to be influenced from your plan by another, you are unable to judge as you should, because you have allowed another's influence to deprive you of your courage and determination without absorbing any of his in return, so you are in much the same predicament as you would be in if you turned over all your worldly possessions to another without getting value received.

Concentrate on just the opposite of fear, want, poverty, sickness, etc. Never doubt your own ability. You have plenty, *if you will just use it*. A great many men are failures because they doubt their own capacity. Instead of building up strong mental forces, which would be of the greatest use to them, their fear thoughts tear them down. Fear paralyzes energy. It keeps us from attracting the forces that make success. Fear is the worst enemy we have.

Few people really know that they can accomplish much. They desire the full extent of their powers, but alas, it is only occasionally that you find a man who is aware of the great possibilities within him. When you believe with all your mind and heart and soul that you can do something, you thereby develop the courage to steadily and confidently live up to that belief. You have now gone a long way towards accomplishing it. Strong courage eliminates the injurious and opposing forces by summoning their masters, the yet-stronger forces that will serve you.

Courage is yours for the asking. All you have to do is to believe in it, claim it, and use it. One man of courage can fire with his spirit a whole army of men, whether military or industrial, because courage, like cowardice, is contagious.

Lesson XII

Concentrate on Wealth

It was never intended that man should be poor. When wealth is obtained under the proper conditions, it broadens the life. Everything has its value. Everything has a good use and a bad use. The forces of mind, like wealth, can be directed either for good or evil. A little rest will re-create forces. Too much rest degenerates into laziness, and brainless, dreamy longings.

So, the first step toward acquiring wealth is to surround yourself with helpful influences; to claim for yourself an environment of culture, place yourself in it, and be molded by its influences.

Wealth is usually the fruit of achievement. It is not, however, altogether the result of being industrious. Thousands of persons work hard who never grow wealthy. Others with much less effort acquire wealth. Seeing possibilities is another step toward acquiring wealth. A man may be as industrious as he can possibly be, but if he does not use his mental forces he will be a laborer, to be directed by the man who uses to good advantage his mental forces.

No one can become wealthy in an ordinary lifetime by mere savings from earnings. Many scrimp and economize all their lives; but by so doing waste all their vitality and energy.

For example, I know a man who used to walk to work. It took him an hour to go and an hour to return. He could have taken a car and gone in twenty minutes. He saved ten cents a day, but wasted an hour and a half. It was not a very profitable investment, unless the time spent in physical exercise yielded him large returns in the way of health.

The same amount of time spent in concentrated effort to overcome his unfavorable business environment might have firmly planted his feet in the path of prosperity.

One of the big mistakes made by many people is that they associate with those who fail to call out or develop the best that is in them. When the social side of life is developed too exclusively, and recreation or entertainment becomes the leading motive of a person's life, he acquires habits of extravagance instead of economy; habits of wasting his resources, physical, mental, moral, and spiritual, instead of conserving them.

The other day I attended a lecture on Prosperity. I knew the lecturer had been practically broke for ten years. I wanted to hear what he had to say. He spoke very well. He no doubt benefited some of his hearers, but he had not profited by his own teachings. I introduced myself and asked him if he believed in his maxims. He said he did. I asked him if they had made him prosperous. He said not exactly. I asked him why. He answered that he thought he was fated not to experience prosperity.

In half an hour, I showed that man why poverty had always been his companion. He had dressed poorly. He held his lectures in poor surroundings. By his actions and beliefs he attracted poverty. He did not realize that his thoughts and his surroundings exercised an unfavorable influence. I said: "Thoughts are moving forces; great powers. Thoughts of wealth attract wealth. Therefore, if you desire wealth you must attract the forces that will help you to secure it. Your thoughts attract a similar kind of thoughts. If you hold thoughts of poverty you attract poverty. If you make up your mind you are going to be wealthy, you will instill this thought into all your mental forces, and you will at the same time use every external condition to help you."

Business success depends on foresight, good judgment, grit, firm resolution, and settled purpose. But never forget that thought is as real a force as electricity. Let your thoughts be such that you will send out as good as you receive; if you do not, you are not enriching others, and therefore deserve not to be enriched.

Again I repeat that the first as well as the last step in acquiring wealth is to surround yourself with good influences—good thought, good health, good home and business environment, and successful business associates. Cultivate, by every legitimate means, the acquaintance of men of big caliber. Bring your thought vibrations in regard to business into harmony with theirs. This will make your society not only agreeable, but sought after, and, when you have formed intimate friendships with clean, reputable men of wealth, entrust to them, for investment, your surplus earnings, however small, until you have developed the initiative and business acumen to successfully manage your own investments. By this time you will, through such associations, have found your place in life which, if you have rightly concentrated upon and used your opportunities, will not be among men of small parts.

There is somewhere in every brain the energy that will get you out of that rut and put you far up on the mountain of success, if you can only use the energy. And hope, self-confidence, and the determination to do something supply the spark that makes the energy work.

Lesson XIII

You Can Concentrate, But Will You?

All have the ability to concentrate, but will you? You can, but whether you will or not depends on you. It is one thing to be able to do something, another to do it. There is far more ability not used than is used. Why do not more men of ability make something of themselves? There are comparatively few successful men, but many ambitious ones. Why do not more get along? Cases may differ, but the fault is usually their own. They have had chances, perhaps better ones than some others that have made good.

What would you like to do that you are not doing? If you think you should be "getting on" better, why don't you? Study yourself carefully. Learn your shortcomings. Sometimes only a mere trifle keeps one from branching out and becoming a success. Discover why you have not been making good—the cause of your failure. Have you been expecting someone to lead you, or to make a way for you? If you have, concentrate on a new line of thought.

There are two things absolutely necessary for success—energy and the will to succeed. Nothing can take the place of either of these.

When we see those with handicaps amounting to something great in the world, the able-bodied man should feel ashamed of himself if he does not make good. There is nothing that can resist the force of perseverance. The way ahead for all of us is not clear sailing, but all hard passages can be bridged.

Many men will not begin an undertaking unless they feel sure they will succeed in it. What a mistake! This would be right, if we were sure of what we could and could not do. But who knows? *There may be an obstruction there now that might not be there next week. There may not be an obstruction there now that will be there next week.* The trouble with most people is that just as soon as they see their way blocked they lose courage. They forget that usually there is a way around the difficulty. It's up to you to find it. If you tackle something with little effort, when the conditions call for a big effort, you will, of course, not win. Tackle everything with a feeling that you will use all the power within you to make it a success. This is the kind of concentrated effort that succeeds.

Most people are beaten before they start. They think they are going to encounter obstacles, and they look for them instead of for means to overcome them. The result is that they increase their obstacles instead of diminishing them. Have you ever undertaken something that you thought would be hard, but afterwards found it easy? That is the way a great many times. Things that look difficult in advance turn out to be easy of conquest when once encountered. So start out on your journey with the idea that the road is going to be clear for you, and that if it is not you will clear the way.

The one great keynote of success is to do whatever you have decided on. Don't be turned from your path, but resolve that you are going to accomplish what you set out to do. Don't be frightened at a few rebuffs, for they cannot stop the man that is determined—the man that knows in his heart that success is only bought by tremendous resolution, by concentrated and whole-hearted effort.

It is not so much skill that wins victories, as it is activity and great determination. There is no such thing as failure for the man who does his best. No matter what you may be working at, don't let this make you lose courage. *The tides are continually changing, and tomorrow or some other day they will turn to your advantage if you are a willing and ambitious worker.* There is nothing that develops you and increases your courage like work. If it were not for work how monotonous life would become!

So I say to the man who wants to advance: "Don't look upon your present position as your permanent one. Keep your eyes open, and add those qualities to your makeup that will assist you when your opportunity comes. Be ever alert and on the watch for opportunities. Remember, we attract what we set our minds on. If we look for opportunities, we find them."

Lesson XIV

The Art of Concentration with Practical Exercises

Select some thought, and see how long you can hold your mind on it. It is well to have a clock at first and keep track of the time. If you decide to think about health, you can get a great deal of good from your thinking besides developing concentration. Think of health as being the greatest blessing in the world. Don't let any other thought drift in. The moment one starts to obtrude, make it get out.

Make it a daily habit of concentrating on this thought for, say, ten minutes. Practice until you can hold it to the exclusion of everything else. You will find it of the greatest value to centralize your thoughts on health. Regardless of your present condition, see yourself as you would like to be, and be blind to everything else. You will find it hard at first to forget your ailments, if you have any, but after a short while you can shut out these negative thoughts and see yourself as you want to be. Each time you concentrate, you form a more perfect image of health, and, as you come into its realization, you become healthy, strong, and wholesome.

I want to impress upon your mind that the habit of forming mental images is of the greatest value. It has always been used by successful men of all ages, but few realize its full importance.

Do you know that you are continually acting according to the images you form? If you allow yourself to mold negative images, you unconsciously build a negative disposition. You will think of poverty, weakness, disease, fear, etc., just as surely as you think of these will your objective life express itself in a like way. Just what we think, we will manifest in the external world.

In deep concentration you become linked with the great creative spirit of the universe, and the creative energy then flows through you, vitalizing your creations into form. In deep concentration your mind becomes attuned with the infinite and registers the cosmic intelligence and receives its messages. You become so full of the cosmic energy that you are flooded with divine power. This is a most desired state. It is then we realize the advantages of being connected with the supra-consciousness. The supra-consciousness registers the higher cosmic vibrations. It is often referred to as the wireless station, the message recorded coming from the universal mind.

Watch yourself during the day and see that your muscles do not become tense or strained. See how easy and relaxed you can keep yourself. See how poised you can be at all times. Cultivate a self-poised manner, instead of a nervous, strained appearance. This mental feeling will improve your carriage and demeanor. Stop all useless gestures and movements of the body. These mean that you have not proper control over your body. After you have acquired this control, notice how "ill-at-ease" people are that have not gained this control.

Get rid of any habit you have of twitching or jerking any part of your body. You will find that you make many involuntary movements. You can quickly stop any of these by merely centering your attention on the thought: "I will not."

No matter what you may be doing, imagine that it is your chief object in life. Imagine you are not interested in anything else in the world but what you are doing. Do not let your attention get away from the work you are at. Your attention will no doubt be rebellious, but control it, and do not let it control you. When once you conquer the rebellious attention, you have achieved a greater victory than you can realize at the time.

By concentration you can control your temper. If you are one of those that flare up at the slightest "provocation" and never try to control yourself, just think this over a minute. Does it do you any good? Do you gain anything by it? Doesn't it put you out of poise for some time? Don't you know that this grows on you, and will eventually make you despised by all that have any dealings with you?

Many of you that read this may think you are not guilty of either of these faults, but if you will carefully watch yourself, you will probably find that you are, and, if so, you will be greatly helped by repeating this affirmation each morning:

"I am going to try today not to make a useless gesture or to worry over trifles, or become nervous or irritable. I intend to be calm, and, no difference what may be the circumstances, I will control myself. Henceforth, I resolve to be free from all signs that show lack of self-control."

Now, a word on needless talking. It seems natural to want to tell others what you know; but, by learning to control these desires, you can wonderfully strengthen your powers of concentration. Remember, you have all you can do to attend to your own business. Do not waste your time in thinking of others, or in gossiping about them.

If, from your own observation, you learn something about another person that is detrimental, keep it to yourself. Your opinion may afterwards turn out to be wrong anyway; but whether right or wrong, you have strengthened your will by controlling your desire to communicate your views.

If you hear good news, resist the desire to tell it to the first person you meet and you will be benefited thereby. It will require the concentration of all your powers of resistance to prohibit the desire to tell. After you feel that you have complete control over your desires, you can then tell your news. But you must be able to suppress the desire to communicate the news until you are fully ready to tell it. Persons that do not possess this power of control over desires are apt to tell things that they should not, thereby often involving both themselves and others in needless trouble.

If you are in the habit of getting excited when you hear unpleasant news, just control yourself and receive it without any exclamation of surprise. Say to yourself, "Nothing is going to cause me to lose my self-control." You will find from experience that this self-control will be worth much to you in business. You will be looked upon as a cool-headed businessman, and this in time becomes a valuable asset. Of course, circumstances alter cases. At times it is necessary to become enthused. But be ever on the lookout for opportunities for the practice of self-control. "He that ruleth his spirit is greater than he that ruleth a city."

Lesson XV

Concentrate So You Will Not Forget

We remember only that which makes a deep impression; hence we must first deepen our impressions by associating in our minds certain ideas that are related to them.

Let's say a wife gives her husband a letter to mail. He does not think about it, but automatically puts it in his pocket and forgets all about it. When the letter was given to him had he said to himself, "I will mail this letter. The box is at the next corner and when I pass it I must drop this letter," it would have enabled him to recall the letter the instant he reached the mailbox.

The same rule holds good in regard to more important things. For example, if you are instructed to drop in and see Mr. Smith while out to lunch today, you will not forget it, if, at the moment the instruction is given, you say to yourself something similar to this: "When I get to the corner of Blank Street, on my way to lunch, I shall turn to the right and call on Mr. Smith." In this way the impression is made, the connection established, and the sight of the associated object recalls the errand.

The important thing to do is to deepen the impression at the very moment it enters your mind. This is made possible not only by concentrating the mind upon the idea itself, but by surrounding it with all possible association of ideas, so that each one will reinforce the others.

The mind is governed by laws of association, such as the law that ideas that enter the mind at the same time emerge at the same time, one assisting in recalling the others. You can train yourself to remember in this way by the concentration of the attention on your purpose, in accordance with the laws of association.

Lesson XVI

How Concentration Can Fulfill Your Desire

"It is a spiritual law that the desire to do necessarily implies the ability to do."

All natural desires can be realized. It would be wrong for the Infinite to create wants that could not be supplied. Man's very soul is in his power to think, and it, therefore, is the essence of all created things. Every instinct of man leads to thought, and in every thought there is great possibility because true thought development, when allied to those mysterious powers which perhaps transcend it, has been the cause of all the world's true progress.

Silent, concentrated thought is more potent than spoken words, for speech distracts from the focusing power of the mind by drawing more and more attention to the without.

Man must learn more and more to depend on himself; to seek more for the Infinite within. It is from this source alone that he gains the power to solve his practical difficulties. No one should give up when there is always the resources of Infinity. The cause of failure is that men search in the wrong direction for success, because they are not conscious of their real powers, which when used are capable of guiding them.

The Infinite within is foreign to those who go through life without developing their spiritual powers. But the Infinite helps only he who helps himself. There is no such thing as a Special "Providence." Man will not receive help from the Infinite except to the extent that he believes and hopes and prays for help from this great source.

Remember that the first step in concentration is to form a Mental Image of what you wish to accomplish. This image becomes a thought-seed that attracts thoughts of a similar nature. Around this thought, when it is once planted in the imagination or creative region of the mind, you group or build associated thoughts, which continue to grow as long as your desire is keen enough to compel close concentration.

Form the habit of thinking of something you wish to accomplish for five minutes each day. Shut every other thought out of consciousness. Be confident that you will succeed; make up your mind that all obstacles will be overcome, and that you can rise above any environment.

A great aid in the development of concentration is to write out your thoughts on that which lies nearest your heart and to continue, little by little, to add to it until you have as nearly as possible exhausted the subject. You will find that each day as you focus your forces on this thought at the center of the stream of consciousness, new plans, ideas, and methods will flash into your mind.

We can attract those things that will help us. Very often we seem to receive help in a miraculous way. It may be slow in coming, but once the silent unseen forces are put into operation, they will bring results so long as we do our part. By forming a strong mental image of your desire, you plant the thought-seed that begins working in your interest and, in time, that desire, if in harmony with your higher nature, will materialize.

It may seem that it would be unnecessary to caution you to concentrate only upon achievement that will be good for you, and work no harm to another, but there are many who forget others and their rights, in their anxiety to achieve success. All good things are possible for you to have, but only as you bring your forces into harmony with that law that requires that we mete out justice to fellow travelers as we journey along life's road. So first think over the thing wanted and if it would be good for you to have. Say: "I want to do this; I am going to work to secure it. The way will be open for me."

If you fully grasp mentally the thought of success and hold it in mind each day, you gradually make a pattern or mold, which in time will materialize. But by all means keep free from doubt and fear, the destructive forces. Never allow these to become associated with your thoughts.

At last you will create the desired conditions, and receive help in many unlooked-for ways that will lift you out of the undesired environment. Life will then seem very different to you, for you will have found happiness through awakening within yourself the power to become the master of circumstances, instead of their slave.

Remember the mystical words of Jesus, the Master: "Whatsoever thing ye desire when ye pray, pray as if ye had already received and ye shall have."

Lesson XVII

Ideals Developed by Concentration

We often hear people spoken of as idealists. The fact is we are all idealists to a certain extent, and upon the ideals we picture depend our ultimate success. You must have the mental image if you are to produce the material thing. Everything is first created in the mind. When you control your thoughts, you become a creator. You receive divine ideas and shape them to your individual needs. All things of this world are to you just what you think they are. Your happiness and success depend upon your ideals.

Concentrate Upon Your Ideals and They Will Become Material Actualities. Through concentration we work out our ideals in physical life. Your future depends upon the ideals you are forming now. Your past ideals are determining your present. Therefore, if you want a bright future, you must begin to prepare for it today.

We say that a man is as changeable as the weather. What is meant is his ideals change. Every time you change your ideal you think differently. You become like a rudderless boat on an ocean. Therefore realize the importance of holding to your ideal until it becomes a reality.

You get up in the morning determined that nothing will make you lose your temper. This is your ideal of a person of real strength and poise. Something takes place that upsets you completely, and you lose your temper. For the time being you forget your ideal. If you had just thought a second of what a well-poised person implies you would not have become angry. *You lose your poise when you forget your ideal.* Each time we allow our ideals to be shattered we also weaken our willpower. Holding to your ideals develops willpower. Never forget this.

Why do so many fail? Because they don't hold to their ideal until it becomes a mental habit. When they concentrate on it to the exclusion of all other things, it becomes a reality. "I am that which I think myself to be."

You must give some hours to concentrated, consistent, persistent thought. You must study yourself and your weaknesses.

No man gets over a fence by wishing himself on the other side. He must climb.

No man gets out of the rut of dull, tiresome, monotonous life by merely wishing himself out of the rut. He must climb.

If you are standing still, or going backward, there is something wrong. You are the person to find out what is wrong.

Don't think that you are neglected, or not understood, or not appreciated.

Such thoughts are the thoughts of failure.

You know that the only thing in the world that you have got to count upon is yourself.

Lesson XVIII
Concentration Reviewed

In this closing chapter, I want to impress you to concentrate on what you do, instead of performing most of your work unconsciously or automatically, until you have formed habits that give you the mastery of your work, and your life powers and forces.

Very often the hardest part of work is thinking about it. When you get right into it, it does not seem so disagreeable. This is the experience of many when they first commence to learn how to concentrate. So never think it a difficult task, but undertake it with the "I Will Spirit," and you will find that its acquirement will be as easy as its application will be useful.

Read the life of any great man, and you will generally find that the dominant quality that made him successful was the ability to concentrate. Study those who have been failures, and you will often find that lack of concentration was the cause.

Never say, "I can't concentrate today." You can do it just the minute you say, "I will." You *can* keep your thoughts from straying, just the same as you can control your arms. Once you realize this fact, you can train the will to concentrate on anything you wish. If it wanders, it is your fault.

You are not using your will. But don't blame it on your will, and say it is weak. The will is the same whether you act as if it were weak or as if it were strong. When you act as if your will is strong you say, "I can." When you act as if it were weak you say, "I can't." It requires the same amount of effort.

Some men get in the habit of thinking, "I can't," and they fail. Others think, "I can," and succeed. So remember, it is for you to decide whether you will join the army of "I can't" or "I can."

The big mistake with so many is that they don't realize that when they say, "I can't," they really say, "I won't try." You cannot tell what you can do until you try. "Can't" means you will not try.

Before going to bed tonight, repeat: "I am going to choose my own thoughts, and to hold them as long as I choose. I am going to shut out all thoughts that weaken or interfere, that make me timid. My Will is as strong as anyone else's." While going to work the next morning, repeat this Keep this up for a month, and you will find you will have a better opinion of yourself. These are the factors that make you a success. Hold fast to them always.

Concentration is nothing but willing to do a certain thing. All foreign thoughts can be kept out by willing that they stay out. You cannot realize your possibilities until you commence to direct your mind.

You have at times been in a position that required courage, and you were surprised at the amount you showed.

Now, when once you arouse yourself, you have this courage all the time and it is not necessary to have a special occasion reveal it. My object in so strongly impressing this on your mind is to make you aware that the same courage, the same determination that you show at certain exceptionable times, you have at your command at all times. It is a part of your vast resources. Use it often and well, in working out the highest destiny of which you are capable.

Father Time keeps going on and on. Every day he rolls around means one less day for you on this planet. Most of us only try to master the external conditions of this world. We think our success and happiness depend on us doing so. These are, of course, important, and I don't want you to think they are not; but I want you to realize that when death comes, only those inherent and acquired qualities and conditions within the mentality—your character, conduct, and soul growth—will go with you. If these are what they should be, you need not be afraid of not being successful and happy, for with these qualities you can mold external materials and conditions.

Now start from this minute to act according to the advice of the higher self in everything you do. If you do, its ever-harmonious forces will necessarily ensure a successful fulfillment of all your life purposes. Whenever you feel tempted to disobey your higher promptings, hold the thought: *"My higher self ensures to me the happiness of doing that which best answers my true relations to all others."*

You possess latent talents, which when developed and used are of assistance to you and others. But if you do not properly use them, you shirk your duty, and you will be the loser and suffer from the consequences. Others will also be worse off if you do not fulfill your obligations.

Hold the thought: *"I will live for my best. I seek wisdom, self-knowledge, happiness and power to help others. I act from the higher self, therefore only the best can come to me."*

The more we become conscious of the presence of the higher self, the more we should try to become a true representative of the human soul in all its wholeness and holiness, instead of wasting our time dwelling on some trifling external quality or defect. We should try to secure a true conception of what we really are so as not to over value the external furnishings. You will then not surrender your dignity or self-respect when others ignorantly make a display of material things to show off. Only the person who realizes that he is a permanent Being knows what the true self is.

About the Author

THERON Q. DUMONT was one of several pseudonyms used by William Walker Atkinson, a popular and innovative New Thought writer and publisher in the early twentieth century. Born in Baltimore, Maryland, in 1862, Atkinson became a successful attorney in 1894. Following a series of illnesses, he immersed himself in New Thought literature. He soon became an important figure in the early days of the movement, publishing magazines such as *Suggestion*, *New Thought*, and *Advanced Thought*. Under the aegis of his own publishing company, Yogi Publication Society, Atkinson wrote many self-bylined works, and many titles under the pseudonyms Yogi Ramacharaka, Magus Incognito, Theron Q. Dumont, and Three Initiates. Under the last of these, Atkinson wrote his most popular and enduring work, *The Kybalion*. Published in 1908 by Atkinson's Chicago-based press, *The Kybalion* is perhaps the most widely read occult book of the twentieth century. Atkinson died in California in 1932.

Power and Wealth

POWER AND WEALTH

*The Immortal Classics on
Will & Money—
Now in Special Condensations*

by Ralph Waldo Emerson

THE CONDENSED CLASSICS LIBRARY™

Contents

INTRODUCTION
Genius and Practicality
by Mitch Horowitz   **197**

I. Power   201

II. Wealth   218

ABOUT THE AUTHOR   237

Introduction

Genius and Practicality
by Mitch Horowitz

Part of Ralph Waldo Emerson's greatness as a writer is that he never shied away from practicality. This was true of his philosophical descendant William James, as well. It can be argued that Emerson's most practical works—which include his essays *Power* and *Wealth*—were not among his greatest. Critic Irving Howe wrote that in such works the philosopher "merely tugs the complexities . . . into the shallows of the explicit."

There is truth in this charge. And yet this judgment fails to take account of Emerson's bravery. Emerson felt obligated to be direct—to provide his readers with plans of action. If this approach reduced philosophical heights, it also banished authorial cowardice. Emerson would not dodge the question of *how* to practice the kinds of self-driven living that his philosophical essays endorsed.

Hence, it is in his essays *Power* and *Wealth*, which Emerson published in *The Conduct of Life* in 1860, that the Transcendentalist prescribed exactly how and under what conditions a person can successfully assert his will in outer life.

In *Power*, Emerson names four essential elements to exercising personal power. The first—and that which sustains all the others—is to be "in sympathy with the course of things." Displaying his innate instinct for Taoism and other Eastern philosophies, Emerson believed that an individual could read the *nature of things* and seek to merge with it, like a twig carried downstream. "The mind that is parallel with the laws of nature," he writes, "will be in the current of events, and strong with their strength."

The second element of power is *health*. Emerson means this on different levels. He is speaking broadly of the vitality of body and spirit; the state of physicality and personal morale that sustains risks, seeks adventure, and completes plans. But he also speaks of routine bodily health, without which the individual's energies are sapped.

The third element is *concentration*. One of nature's laws is that concentration of energies brings impact. The concentration of a striking blow delivers the greatest force. Too often we deplete our energies by dispersing or spreading thin our aims and efforts. In *Power*, an imaginary oracle says: "Enlarge not thy destiny, endeavor not to do more than is given thee in charge." Like light focused in a laser, concentration into a single beam brings the greatest power.

The fourth and final element of power is *drilling*. By this Emerson means repeating a practice over and over until you can perform it with excellence. The martial artist repeats his movements and routines to the point where they enter his physical memory and are available to him under all conditions. Likewise, we must drill—or practice or rehearse—to the point where we have mastered our chosen task.

In the essay *Wealth*, Emerson declares, chin out, that the individual is "born to be rich." And by riches, the philosopher is not employing a coy metaphor. He means cold, hard cash. But he also identifies accumulation of capital as befitting only that person who uses it to productive ends. Emerson writes,

> *Every man is a consumer, and ought to be a producer. He fails to make his place good in the world, unless he not only pays his debt, but also adds something to the common wealth. Nor can he do justice to his genius, without making some larger demand on the world than a bare subsistence. He is by constitution expensive, and needs to be rich.*

Only those purchases that expand your power and abilities, he writes, leave you any richer. Indeed, wealth that fails to accompany expansion is wealth thrown away. "Nor is the man enriched," Emerson writes, "in repeating the old experiments of animal sensation." Rather, you are enriched when you increase your ability to earn, to do, and to grow. Wealth, properly understood, is power. That is why these essays are conjoined.

So, how do you earn wealth? Emerson outlines roughly three steps: 1) First filling some nonnegotiable, subsistence-level need in your own life: this what drove the primeval farmers, hunter-gathers, and villagers. 2) Next, applying one's particular talents to nature, and expansively filling the needs of others. If you do not know or understand your talents, you must start there before anything is possible. Your particular talent is a source of excellence. And, finally, 3) using your wealth for the purposes of productiveness: paying down debts, making compound investments, and procuring the tools and talents of your trade. Building and expanding is the only sound way to riches. And such things also reflect your code and fiber as a progressing being.

By entering the mechanics of practicality, did Emerson sacrifice some of his transcendental splendor? Some thought so; I see it differently. If Emerson had avoided such an approach he would have been guilty of failing to take his philosophy onto the road. Complexity does not excuse inaction. And here I am reminded of an observation by the flawed and brilliant poet Ezra Pound, to whom I cede the last word: "But to have done instead of not doing/ This is not vanity."

I. Power

Who shall set a limit to the influence of a human being? There are men, who, by their sympathetic attractions, carry nations with them, and lead the activity of the human race. And if there be such a tie, that, wherever the mind of man goes, nature will accompany him, perhaps there are men whose magnetisms are of that force to draw material and elemental powers, and, where they appear, immense instrumentalities organize around them. Life is a search after power; and this is an element with which the world is so saturated,—there is no chink or crevice in which it is not lodged,—that no honest seeking goes unrewarded. A man should prize events and possessions as the ore in which this fine mineral is found; and he can well afford to let events and possessions, and the breath of the body go, if their value has been added to him in the shape of power. If he have secured the elixir, he can spare the wide gardens from which it was distilled. A cultivated man, wise to know and bold to perform, is the end to which nature works, and the education of the will is the flowering and result of all this geology and astronomy.

All successful men have agreed in one thing,—they were *causationists*. They believed that things went not by luck, but by law; that there was not a weak or a cracked link in the chain that joins the first and last of things. A belief in causality, or strict connection between every trifle and the principle of being, and, in consequence, belief in compensation, or, that nothing is got for nothing,— characterizes all valuable minds, and must control every effort that is made by an industrious one. The most valiant men are the best believers in the tension of the laws. "All the great captains," said Bonaparte, "have performed vast achievements by conforming with the rules of the art,—by adjusting efforts to obstacles."

The key to the age may be this, or that, or the other, as the young orators describe—the key to all ages is—Imbecility; imbecility in the vast majority of men, at all times, and, even in heroes, in all but certain eminent moments; victims of gravity, custom, and fear. This gives force to the strong,—that the multitude have no habit of self-reliance or original action.

We must reckon success a constitutional trait. Courage—the old physicians taught, (and their meaning holds, if their physiology is a little mythical,)—courage, or the degree of life, is as the degree of circulation of the blood in the arteries. Where the arteries hold their blood, is courage and adventure possible. Where they pour it unrestrained into the veins, the spirit is low and feeble. For performance of great mark, it needs extraordinary health. If

Eric is in robust health, and has slept well, and is at the top of his condition, and thirty years old, at his departure from Greenland, he will steer west, and his ships will reach Newfoundland. But take out Eric, and put in a stronger and bolder man,—Biorn, or Thorfin,—and the ships will, with just as much ease, sail six hundred, one thousand, fifteen hundred miles further, and reach Labrador and New England. There is no chance in results. With adults, as with children, one class enter cordially into the game, and whirl with the whirling world; the others have cold hands, and remain bystanders; or are only dragged in by the humor and vivacity of those who can carry a dead weight. The first wealth is health. Sickness is poor-spirited, and cannot serve any one: it must husband its resources to live. But health or fullness answers its own ends, and has to spare, runs over, and inundates the neighborhoods and creeks of other men's necessities.

All power is of one kind, a sharing of the nature of the world. The mind that is parallel with the laws of nature will be in the current of events, and strong with their strength. One man is made of the same stuff of which events are made; is in sympathy with the course of things; can predict it. Whatever befalls, befalls him first; so that he is equal to whatever shall happen. A man who knows men, can talk well on politics, trade, law, war, religion. For, everywhere, men are led in the same manners.

The advantage of a strong pulse is not to be supplied by any labor, art, or concert. It is like the climate, which easily rears a crop, which no glass, or irrigation, or tillage, or manures, can elsewhere rival. It is like the opportunity of a city like New York, or Constantinople, which needs no diplomacy to force capital or genius or labor to it. They come of themselves, as the waters flow to it.

This affirmative force is in one, and is not in another, as one horse has the spring in him, and another in the whip. "On the neck of the young man," said Hafiz, "sparkles no gem so gracious as enterprise." Import into any stationary district, as into an old Dutch population in New York or Pennsylvania, or among the planters of Virginia, a colony of hardy Yankees, with seething brains, heads full of steam-hammer, pulley, crank, and toothed wheel,—and everything begins to shine with values. In every company, there is not only the active and passive sex, but, in both men and women, a deeper and more important *sex of mind*, namely, the inventive or creative class of both men and women, and the uninventive or accepting class. Each plus man represents his set, and, if he have the accidental advantage of personal ascendency,—which implies neither more nor less of talent, but merely the temperamental or taming eye of a soldier or a schoolmaster, (which one has, and one has not, as one has a black moustache and one a blond,) then quite easily and without envy or resistance, all his coadjutors and feeders will admit his right to absorb them.

There is always room for a man of force, and he makes room for many. Society is a troop of thinkers, and the best heads among them take the best places. A feeble man can see the farms that are fenced and tilled, the houses that are built. The strong man sees the possible houses and farms. His eye makes estates, as fast as the sun breeds clouds.

When a new boy comes into school, when a man travels, and encounters strangers every day, or, when into any old club a new comer is domesticated, that happens which befalls, when a strange ox is driven into a pen or pasture where cattle are kept; there is at once a trial of strength between the best pair of horns and the new comer, and it is settled thenceforth which is the leader. So now, there is a measuring of strength, very courteous, but decisive, and an acquiescence thenceforward when these two meet. Each reads his fate in the other's eyes. The weaker party finds, that none of his information or wit quite fits the occasion. He thought he knew this or that: he finds that he omitted to learn the end of it. Nothing that he knows will quite hit the mark, whilst all the rival's arrows are good, and well thrown. But if he knew all the facts in the encyclopaedia, it would not help him: for this is an affair of presence of mind, of attitude, of aplomb: the opponent has the sun and wind, and, in every cast, the choice of weapon and mark; and, when he himself is matched with some other antagonist, his own shafts fly well and hit. 'Tis a question of stomach and constitution. The second man is as good as the first,—perhaps better; but has not stoutness or stomach, as the first has, and so his wit seems over-fine or under-fine.

Health is good,—power, life, that resists disease, poison, and all enemies, and is conservative, as well as creative.

Vivacity, leadership, must be had, and we are not allowed to be nice in choosing. And we have a certain instinct, that where is great amount of life, though gross and peccant, it has its own checks and purifications, and will be found at last in harmony with moral laws.

We prosper with such vigor, that, like thrifty trees, which grow in spite of ice, lice, mice, and borers, so we do not suffer from the profligate swarms. The huge animals nourish huge parasites, and the rancor of the disease attests the strength of the constitution.

All kinds of power usually emerge at the same time; good energy, and bad; power of mind, with physical health; the ecstasies of devotion, with the exasperations of debauchery. The same elements are always present, only sometimes these conspicuous, and sometimes those; what was yesterday foreground, being to-day background—what was surface, playing now a not less effective part as basis. The longer the drought lasts, the more is the atmosphere surcharged with water. The faster the ball falls to the sun, the force to fly off is by so much augmented. And, in morals, wild liberty breeds iron conscience; natures with great impulses have great resources, and return from far. In politics, the sons of democrats will be whigs; whilst red republicanism, in the father, is a spasm of nature to engender an intolerable tyrant in the next age. On the other hand, conservatism, ever more timorous and narrow, disgusts the children, and drives them for a mouthful of fresh air into radicalism.

Those who have most of this coarse energy,—the 'bruisers,' who have run the gauntlet of caucus and tavern through the county or the state, have their own vices, but they have the good nature of strength and courage. Fierce and unscrupulous, they are usually frank and direct, and above falsehood. Our politics fall into bad hands, and churchmen and men of refinement, it seems agreed, are not fit persons to send to Congress. Politics is a deleterious profession, like some poisonous handicrafts. Men in power have no opinions, but may be had cheap for any opinion, for any purpose,—and if it be only a question between the most civil and the most forcible, I lean to the last.

In trade, also, this energy usually carries a trace of ferocity. Philanthropic and religious bodies do not commonly make their executive officers out of saints. The communities hitherto founded by Socialists,—the Jesuits, the Port-Royalists, the American communities at New Harmony, at Brook Farm, at Zoar, are only possible, by installing Judas as steward. The rest of the offices may be filled by good burgesses. The pious and charitable proprietor has a foreman not quite so pious and charitable. The most amiable of country gentlemen has a certain pleasure in the teeth of the bull-dog which guards his orchard. Of the Shaker society, it was formerly a sort of proverb in the country, that they always sent the devil to market. And in representations of the Deity, painting, poetry, and popular religion have ever drawn the wrath from Hell. It is an esoteric doctrine of society, that a little wickedness is good to make muscle; as if conscience were not good for hands and legs, as if poor decayed formalists of law and order cannot run like wild goats, wolves, and conies; that, as there is a use in medicine for poisons, so the world cannot move without rogues; that public spirit and the ready hand are as well found among the malignants. 'Tis not very rare, the coincidence of sharp private and political practice, with public spirit, and good neighborhood.

Whilst thus the energy for originating and executing work, deforms itself by excess, and so our axe chops off our own fingers,—this evil is not without remedy. All the elements whose aid man calls in, will sometimes become his masters, especially those of most subtle force. Shall he, then, renounce steam, fire, and electricity, or, shall he learn to deal with them? The rule for this whole class of agencies is,—all plus is good; only put it in the right place.

Men of this surcharge of arterial blood cannot live on nuts, herb-tea, and elegies; cannot read novels, and play whist; cannot satisfy all their wants at the Thursday Lecture, or the Boston Athenaeum. They pine for adventure, and must go to Pike's Peak; had rather die by the hatchet of a Pawnee, than sit all day and every day at a counting-room desk. They are made for war, for the sea, for mining, hunting, and clearing; for hair-breadth adventures, huge risks, and the joy of eventful living. Some men cannot endure an hour of calm at sea.

The excess of virility has the same importance in general history, as in private and industrial life. Strong race or strong individual rests at last on natural forces, which are best in the savage, who, like the beasts around him, is still in reception of the milk from the teats of Nature. Cut off the connection between any of our works, and this aboriginal source, and the work is shallow. The people lean on this, and the mob is not quite so bad an argument as we sometimes say, for it has this good side. "March without the people," said a French deputy from the tribune, "and you march into night: their instincts are a finger-pointing of Providence, always turned toward real benefit."

The best anecdotes of this force are to be had from savage life, in explorers, soldiers, and buccaneers. But who cares for fallings-out of assassins, and fights of bears, or grindings of icebergs? Physical force has no value, where there is nothing else. Snow in snow-banks, fire in volcanoes and solfataras is cheap. The luxury of ice is in tropical countries, and midsummer days. The luxury of fire is, to have a little on our hearth: and of electricity, not volleys of the charged cloud, but the manageable stream on the battery-wires.

In history, the great moment is, when the savage is just ceasing to be a savage, with all his hairy Pelasgic strength directed on his sense of beauty;—and you have Pericles and Phidias,—not yet passed over into the Corinthian civility. Everything good in nature and the world is in that moment of transition, when the swarthy juices still flow plentifully from nature, but their astringency or acridity is got out by ethics and humanity.

The triumphs of peace have been in some proximity to war. Whilst the hand was still familiar with the sword-hilt, whilst the habits of the camp were still visible in the port and complexion of the gentleman, his intellectual power culminated: the compression and tension of these stern conditions is a training for the finest and softest arts, and can rarely be compensated in tranquil times, except by some analogous vigor drawn from occupations as hardy as war.

We say that success is constitutional; depends on a *plus* condition of mind and body, on power of work, on courage; that it is of main efficacy in carrying on the world, and, though rarely found in the right state for an article of commerce, but oftener in the supersaturate or excess, which makes it dangerous and destructive, yet it cannot be spared, and must be had in that form, and absorbents provided to take off its edge.

The affirmative class monopolize the homage of mankind. They originate and execute all the great feats. What a force was coiled up in the skull of Napoleon! Of the sixty thousand men making his army at Eylau, it seems some thirty thousand were thieves and burglars. The men whom, in peaceful communities, we hold if we can, with iron at their legs, in prisons, under the muskets of sentinels, this man dealt with, hand to hand, dragged them to their duty, and won his victories by their bayonets.

This aboriginal might gives a surprising pleasure when it appears under conditions of supreme refinement, as in the proficients in high art. When Michel Angelo was forced to paint the Sistine Chapel in fresco, of which art he knew nothing, he went down into the Pope's gardens behind the Vatican, and with a shovel dug out ochres, red and yellow, mixed them with glue and water with his own hands, and having, after many trials, at last suited himself, climbed his ladders, and painted away, week after week, month after month, the sibyls and prophets. He surpassed his successors in rough vigor, as much as in purity of intellect and refinement. He was not crushed by his one picture left unfinished at last. Michel was wont to draw his figures first in skeleton, then to clothe them with flesh, and lastly to drape them. "Ah!" said a brave painter to me, thinking on these things, "if a man has failed, you will find he has dreamed instead of working. There is no way to success in our art, but to take off your coat, grind paint, and work like a digger on the railroad, all day and every day."

Success goes thus invariably with a certain *plus* or positive power: an ounce of power must balance an ounce of weight. And, though a man cannot return into his mother's womb, and be born with new amounts of vivacity, yet there are two economies, which are the best *succedanea* which the case admits. The first is, the stopping off decisively our miscellaneous activity, and concentrating our force on one or a few points; as the gardener, by severe pruning, forces the sap of the tree into one or two vigorous limbs, instead of suffering it to spindle into a sheaf of twigs.

"Enlarge not thy destiny," said the oracle: "endeavor not to do more than is given thee in charge." The one prudence in life is concentration; the one evil is dissipation: and it makes no difference whether our dissipations are coarse or fine; property and its cares, friends, and a social habit, or politics, or music, or feasting. Everything is good which takes away one plaything and delusion more, and drives us home to add one stroke of faithful work. Friends, books, pictures, lower duties, talents, flatteries, hopes,—all are distractions which cause oscillations in our giddy balloon, and make a good poise and a straight course impossible. You must elect your work; you shall take what your brain can, and drop all the rest. Only so, can that amount of vital force accumulate, which can make the step from knowing to doing. No matter how much faculty of idle seeing a man has, the step from knowing to doing is rarely taken. 'Tis a step out of a chalk circle of imbecility into fruitfulness. Many an artist lacking this, lacks all: he sees the masculine Angelo or Cellini with despair. He, too, is up to Nature and the First Cause in his thought. But the spasm to collect and swing his whole being into one act, he has not. The poet Campbell said, that "a man accustomed to work was equal to any achievement he resolved on, and, that, for himself, necessity not inspiration was the prompter of his muse."

Concentration is the secret of strength in politics, in war, in trade, in short, in all management of human affairs. One of the high anecdotes of the world is the reply of Newton to the inquiry, "how he had been able to achieve his discoveries?"—"By always intending my mind." Or if you will have a text from politics, take this from Plutarch: "There was, in the whole city, but one street in which Pericles was ever seen, the street which led to the market-place and the council house. He declined all invitations to banquets, and all gay assemblies and company. During the whole period of his administration, he never dined at the table of a friend." Or if we seek an example from trade,—"I hope," said a good man to Rothschild, "your children are not too fond of money and business: I am sure you would not wish that."—"I am sure I should wish that: I wish them to give mind, soul, heart, and body to business,—that is the way to be happy. It requires a great deal of boldness and a great deal of caution, to make a great fortune, and when you have got it, it requires ten times as much wit to keep it. If I were to listen to all the projects proposed to me, I should ruin myself very soon. Stick to one business, young man. Stick to your brewery, and you will be the great brewer of London. Be brewer, and banker, and merchant, and manufacturer, and you will soon be in the Gazette."

Many men are knowing, many are apprehensive and tenacious, but they do not rush to a decision. But in our flowing affairs a decision must be made,—the best, if you can; but any is better than none. There are twenty ways of going to a point, and one is the shortest; but set out at once on one. A man who has that presence of mind which can bring to him on the instant all he knows, is worth for action a dozen men who know as much, but can only bring it to light slowly. The good Speaker in the House is not the man who knows the theory of parliamentary tactics, but the man who decides off-hand. The good judge is not he who does hair-splitting justice to every allegation, but who, aiming at substantial justice, rules something intelligible for the guidance of suitors. The good lawyer is not the man who has an eye to every side and angle of contingency, and qualifies all his qualifications, but who throws himself on your part so heartily, that he can get you out of a scrape. Dr. Johnson said, in one of his flowing sentences, "Miserable beyond all names of wretchedness is that unhappy pair, who are doomed to reduce beforehand to the principles of abstract reason all the details of each domestic day. There are cases where little can be said, and much must be done."

The second substitute for temperament is drill, the power of use and routine. The hack is a better roadster than the Arab barb. In chemistry, the galvanic stream, slow, but continuous, is equal in power to the electric spark, and is, in our arts, a better agent. So in human action, against the spasm of energy, we offset the continuity of drill. We spread the same amount of force over much time, instead of condensing it into a moment. 'Tis the same ounce of gold here in a ball, and there in a leaf. At West Point, Col. Buford, the chief engineer, pounded with a hammer on the trunnions of a cannon, until he broke them off. He fired a piece of ordnance some hundred times in swift succession, until it burst. Now which stroke broke the trunnion? Every stroke. Which blast burst the piece? Every blast. The worst provincial company of actors would go through a play better than the best amateur company. The worst regular troops will beat the best volunteers. Practice is nine tenths. A course of mobs is good practice for orators. All the great speakers were bad speakers at first. Stumping it through England for seven years, made Cobden a consummate debater. Stumping it through New England for twice seven, trained Wendell Phillips. The way to learn German, is, to read the same dozen pages over and over a hundred times, till you know every word and particle in them, and can pronounce and repeat them by heart. No genius can recite a ballad at first reading, so well as mediocrity can at the fifteenth or twentieth reading. A humorous friend of mine thinks, that the reason why Nature is so perfect in her art, and gets up such inconceivably fine sunsets, is, that she has learned how, at last, by dint of doing the same thing so very often. Cannot one converse better on a topic on which he has experience, than on one which is new? Hence the use of drill, and the worthlessness of amateurs to cope with practitioners. Six hours every day at the piano, only to give facility of touch; six hours a day at painting, only to give command of the odious materials, oil, ochres, and brushes. The masters say, that they know a master in music, only by seeing the pose of the hands on the keys;— so difficult and vital an act is the command of the instrument. To have learned the use of the tools, by thousands of manipulations; to have learned the arts of reckoning, by endless adding and dividing, is the power of the mechanic and the clerk.

I remarked in England, in confirmation of a frequent experience at home, that, in literary circles, the men of trust and consideration, bookmakers, editors, university deans and professors, bishops, too, were by no means men of the largest literary talent, but usually of a low and ordinary intellectuality, with a sort of mercantile activity and working talent. Indifferent hacks and mediocrities tower, by pushing their forces to a lucrative point, or by working power, over multitudes of superior men.

I have not forgotten that there are sublime considerations which limit the value of talent and superficial success. We can easily overpraise the vulgar hero. There are sources on which we have not drawn. I know what I abstain from. But this force or spirit, being the means relied on by Nature for bringing the work of the day about,—as far as we attach importance to household life, and the prizes of the world, we must respect that. And I hold, that an economy may be applied to it; it is as much a subject of exact law and arithmetic as fluids and gases are; it may be husbanded, or wasted; every man is efficient only as he is a container or vessel of this force, and never was any signal act or achievement in history, but by this expenditure. This is not gold, but the gold-maker; not the fame, but the exploit.

If these forces and this husbandry are within reach of our will, and the laws of them can be read, we infer that all success, and all conceivable benefit for man, is also, first or last, within his reach, and has its own sublime economies by which it may be attained. The world is mathematical, and has no casualty, in all its vast and flowing curve. Success has no more eccentricity, than the gingham and muslin we weave in our mills. I know no more affecting lesson to our busy, plotting New England brains, than to go into one of the factories with which we have lined all the watercourses in the States. A man hardly knows how much he is a machine, until he begins to make telegraph, loom, press, and locomotive, in his own image. But in these, he is forced to leave out his follies and hindrances, so that when we go to the mill, the machine is more moral than we. Let a man dare go to a loom, and see if he be equal to it. Let machine confront machine, and see how they come out. The world-mill is more complex than the calico-mill, and the architect stooped less. In the gingham-mill, a broken thread or a shred spoils the web through a piece of a hundred yards, and is traced back to the girl that wove it, and lessens her wages. The stockholder, on being shown this, rubs his hands with delight. Are you so cunning, Mr. Profitloss, and do you expect to swindle your master and employer, in the web you weave? A day is a more magnificent cloth than any muslin, the mechanism that makes it is infinitely cunninger, and you shall not conceal the sleezy, fraudulent, rotten hours you have slipped into the piece, nor fear that any honest thread, or straighter steel, or more inflexible shaft, will not testify in the web.

II. Wealth

As soon as a stranger is introduced into any company, one of the first questions which all wish to have answered, is, How does that man get his living? And with reason. He is no whole man until he knows how to earn a blameless livelihood. Society is barbarous, until every industrious man can get his living without dishonest customs.

Every man is a consumer, and ought to be a producer. He fails to make his place good in the world, unless he not only pays his debt, but also adds something to the common wealth. Nor can he do justice to his genius, without making some larger demand on the world than a bare subsistence. He is by constitution expensive, and needs to be rich.

Wealth has its source in applications of the mind to nature, from the rudest strokes of spade and axe, up to the last secrets of art. Intimate ties subsist between thought and all production; because a better order is equivalent to vast amounts of brute labor. The forces and the resistances are Nature's, but the mind acts in bringing things from where they abound to where they are wanted; in wise combining; in directing the practice of the useful arts, and in the creation of finer values, by fine art, by eloquence, by song, or the reproductions of memory. Wealth is in applications of mind to nature; and the art of getting rich consists not in industry, much less in saving, but in a better order, in timeliness, in being at the right spot. One man has stronger arms, or longer legs; another sees by the course of streams, and growth of markets, where land will be wanted, makes a clearing to the river, goes to sleep, wakes up rich. Steam is no stronger now, than it was a hundred years ago; but is put to better use. A clever fellow was acquainted with the expansive force of steam; he also saw the wealth of wheat and grass rotting in Michigan. Then he cunningly screws on the steam-pipe to the wheat-crop. Puff now, O Steam! The steam puffs and expands as before, but this time it is dragging all Michigan at its back to hungry New York and hungry England. Coal lay in ledges under the ground since the Flood, until a laborer with pick and windlass brings it to the surface. We may well call it black diamonds. Every basket is power and civilization. For coal is a portable climate. It carries the heat of the tropics to Labrador and the polar circle: and it is the means of transporting itself whithersoever it is wanted. Watt and Stephenson whispered in the ear of mankind their secret, that *a half-ounce of coal will draw two tons a mile*, and coal carries coal, by rail and by boat, to make Canada as warm as Calcutta, and with its comfort brings its industrial power.

When the farmer's peaches are taken from under the tree, and carried into town, they have a new look, and a hundredfold value over the fruit which grew on the same bough, and lies fulsomely on the ground. The craft of the merchant is this bringing a thing from where it abounds, to where it is costly.

Wealth begins in a tight roof that keeps the rain and wind out; in a good pump that yields you plenty of sweet water; in two suits of clothes, so to change your dress when you are wet; in dry sticks to burn; in a good double-wick lamp; and three meals; in a horse, or a locomotive, to cross the land; in a boat to cross the sea; in tools to work with; in books to read; and so, in giving, on all sides, by tools and auxiliaries, the greatest possible extension to our powers, as if it added feet, and hands, and eyes, and blood, length to the day, and knowledge, and good-will.

Wealth begins with these articles of necessity. And here we must recite the iron law which Nature thunders in these northern climates. First, she requires that each man should feed himself. If, happily, his fathers have left him no inheritance, he must go to work, and by making his wants less, or his gains more, he must draw himself out of that state of pain and insult in which she forces the beggar to lie. She gives him no rest until this is done: she starves, taunts, and torments him, takes away warmth, laughter, sleep, friends, and daylight, until he has fought his way to his own loaf. Then, less peremptorily, but still with sting enough, she urges him to the acquisition of such things as belong to him. Every warehouse and shop-window, every fruit-tree, every thought of every hour, opens a new want to him, which it concerns his power and dignity to gratify. It is of no use to argue the wants down: the philosophers have laid the greatness of man in making his wants few; but will a man content himself with a hut and a handful of dried pease? He is born to be rich. He is thoroughly related; and is tempted out by his appetites and fancies to the conquest of this and that piece of nature, until he finds his well-being in the use of his planet, and of more planets than his own. Wealth requires, besides the crust of bread and the roof,—the freedom of the city, the freedom of the earth, travelling, machinery, the benefits of science, music, and fine arts, the best culture, and the best company. He is the rich man who can avail himself of all men's faculties. He is the richest man who knows how to draw a benefit from the labors of the greatest number of men, of men in distant countries, and in past times. The same correspondence that is between thirst in the stomach, and water in the spring, exists between the whole of man and the whole of nature. The elements offer their service to him. The sea, washing the equator and the poles, offers its perilous aid, and the power and empire that follow it,—day by day to his craft and audacity. "Beware of me," it says, "but if you can hold me, I am the key to all the lands." Fire offers, on its side, an equal power. Fire, steam, lightning, gravity, ledges of rock, mines of iron, lead, quicksilver, tin, and gold; forests of all woods; fruits of all climates; animals of all habits; the powers of tillage; the fabrics of his chemic laboratory; the webs of his loom; the masculine draught of his locomotive, the talismans of the machine-shop; all grand and subtile things, minerals, gases, ethers, passions, war, trade, government, are his natural playmates, and, according to the excellence of the machinery in each human being, is his attraction for the instruments he is to employ. The world is his tool-chest, and he is successful, or his education is carried on just so far, as is the marriage of his faculties with nature, or, the degree in which he takes up things into himself.

The strong race is strong on these terms. The Saxons are the merchants of the world; now, for a thousand years, the leading race, and by nothing more than their quality of personal independence, and, in its special modification, pecuniary independence. No reliance for bread and games on the government, no clanship, no patriarchal style of living by the revenues of a chief, no marrying-on,—no system of clientship suits them; but every man must pay his scot. The English are prosperous and peaceable, with their habit of considering that every man must take care of himself, and has himself to thank, if he do not maintain and improve his position in society.

The subject of economy mixes itself with morals, inasmuch as it is a peremptory point of virtue that a man's independence be secured. Poverty demoralizes. A man in debt is so far a slave; and Wall-street thinks it easy for a millionaire to be a man of his word, a man of honor, but, that, in failing circumstances, no man can be relied on to keep his integrity. And when one observes in the hotels and palaces of our Atlantic capitals, the habit of expense, the riot of the senses, the absence of bonds, clanship, fellow-feeling of any kind, he feels, that, when a man or a woman is driven to the wall, the chances of integrity are frightfully diminished, as if virtue were coming to be a luxury which few could afford, or, as Burke said, "at a market almost too high for humanity." He may fix his inventory of necessities and of enjoyments on what scale he pleases, but if he wishes the power and privilege of thought, the chalking out his own career, and having society on his own terms, he must bring his wants within his proper power to satisfy.

The manly part is to do with might and main what you can do. The world is full of fops who never did anything, and who have persuaded beauties and men of genius to wear their fop livery, and these will deliver the fop opinion, that it is not respectable to be seen earning a living; that it is much more respectable to spend without earning; and this doctrine of the snake will come also from the elect sons of light; for wise men are not wise at all hours, and will speak five times from their taste or their humor, to once from their reason. The brave workman, who might betray his feeling of it in his manners, if he do not succumb in his practice, must replace the grace or elegance forfeited, by the merit of the work done. No matter whether he make shoes, or statues, or laws. It is the privilege of any human work which is well done to invest the doer with a certain haughtiness. He can well afford not to conciliate, whose faithful work will answer for him. The mechanic at his bench carries a quiet heart and assured manners, and deals on even terms with men of any condition. The artist has made his picture so true, that it disconcerts criticism. The statue is so beautiful, that it contracts no stain from the market, but makes the market a silent gallery for itself. The case of the young lawyer was pitiful to disgust,—a paltry matter of buttons or tweezer-cases; but the determined youth saw in it an aperture to insert his dangerous wedges, made the insignificance of the thing forgotten, and gave fame by his sense and energy to the name and affairs of the Tittleton snuffbox factory.

Society in large towns is babyish, and wealth is made a toy. The life of pleasure is so ostentatious, that a shallow observer must believe that this is the agreed best use of wealth, and, whatever is pretended, it ends in cosseting. But, if this were the main use of surplus capital, it would bring us to barricades, burned towns, and tomahawks, presently. Men of sense esteem wealth to be the assimilation of nature to themselves, the converting of the sap and juices of the planet to the incarnation and nutriment of their design. Power is what they want,—not candy;—power to execute their design, power to give legs and feet, form and actuality to their thought, which, to a clear-sighted man, appears the end for which the Universe exists, and all its resources might be well applied. Columbus thinks that the sphere is a problem for practical navigation, as well as for closet geometry, and looks on all kings and peoples as cowardly landsmen, until they dare fit him out. Few men on the planet have more truly belonged to it. But he was forced to leave much of his map blank. His successors inherited his map, and inherited his fury to complete it.

So the men of the mine, telegraph, mill, map, and survey,—the monomaniacs, who talk up their project in marts, and offices, and entreat men to subscribe:—how did our factories get built? how did North America get netted with iron rails, except by the importunity of these orators, who dragged all the prudent men in? Is party the madness of many for the gain of a few? This speculative genius is the madness of few for the gain of the world. The projectors are sacrificed, but the public is the gainer. Each of these idealists, working after his thought, would make it tyrannical, if he could. He is met and antagonized by other speculators, as hot as he. The equilibrium is preserved by these counteractions, as one tree keeps down another in the forest, that it may not absorb all the sap in the ground. And the supply in nature of railroad presidents, copper-miners, grand-junctioners, smoke-burners, fire-annihilators, &c., is limited by the same law which keeps the proportion in the supply of carbon, of alum, and of hydrogen.

To be rich is to have a ticket of admission to the master-works and chief men of each race. It is to have the sea, by voyaging; to visit the mountains, Niagara, the Nile, the desert, Rome, Paris, Constantinople; to see galleries, libraries, arsenals, manufactories. The reader of Humboldt's "Cosmos" follows the marches of a man whose eyes, ears, and mind are armed by all the science, arts, and implements which mankind have anywhere accumulated, and who is using these to add to the stock. So is it with Denon, Beckford, Belzoni, Wilkinson, Layard, Kane, Lepsius, and Livingston. "The rich man," says Saadi, "is everywhere expected and at home." The rich take up something more of the world into man's life. They include the country as well as the town, the ocean-side, the White Hills, the Far West, and the old European homesteads of man, in their notion of available material. The world is his, who has money to go over it. He arrives at the sea-shore, and a sumptuous ship has floored and carpeted for him the stormy Atlantic, and made it a luxurious hotel, amid the horrors of tempests. The Persians say, "'Tis the same to him who wears a shoe, as if the whole earth were covered with leather."

Kings are said to have long arms, but every man should have long arms, and should pluck his living, his instruments, his power, and his knowing, from the sun, moon, and stars. Is not then the demand to be rich legitimate? Yet, I have never seen a rich man. I have never seen a man as rich as all men ought to be, or, with an adequate command of nature. The pulpit and the press have many commonplaces denouncing the thirst for wealth; but if men should take these moralists at their word, and leave off aiming to be rich, the moralists would rush to rekindle at all hazards this love of power in the people, lest civilization should be undone. Men are urged by their ideas to acquire the command over nature. Ages derive a culture from the wealth of Roman Caesars, Leo Tenths, magnificent Kings of France, Grand Dukes of Tuscany, Dukes of Devonshire, Townleys, Vernons, and Peels, in England; or whatever great proprietors. It is the interest of all men, that there should be Vaticans and Louvres full of noble works of art; British Museums, and French Gardens of Plants, Philadelphia Academies of Natural History, Bodleian, Ambrosian, Royal, Congressional Libraries. It is the interest of all that there should be Exploring Expeditions; Captain Cooks to voyage round the world, Rosses, Franklins, Richardsons, and Kanes, to find the magnetic and the geographic poles. We are all richer for the measurement of a degree of latitude on the earth's surface. Our navigation is safer for the chart. How intimately our knowledge of the system of the Universe rests on that!—and a true economy in a state or an individual will forget its frugality in behalf of claims like these.

Whilst it is each man's interest, that, not only ease and convenience of living, but also wealth or surplus product should exist somewhere, it need not be in his hands. Often it is very undesirable to him. Goethe said well, "nobody should be rich but those who understand it." Some men are born to own, and can animate all their possessions. Others cannot: their owning is not graceful; seems to be a compromise of their character: they seem to steal their own dividends. They should own who can administer; not they who hoard and conceal; not they who, the greater proprietors they are, are only the greater beggars, but they whose work carves out work for more, opens a path for all. For he is the rich man in whom the people are rich, and he is the poor man in whom the people are poor: and how to give all access to the masterpieces of art and nature, is the problem of civilization. The socialism of our day has done good service in setting men on thinking how certain civilizing benefits, now only enjoyed by the opulent, can be enjoyed by all. For example, the providing to each man the means and apparatus of science, and of the arts. There are many articles good for occasional use, which few men are able to own. Every man wishes to see the ring of Saturn, the satellites and belts of Jupiter and Mars; the mountains and craters in the moon: yet how few can buy a telescope! and of those, scarcely one would like the trouble of keeping it in order, and exhibiting it. So of electrical and chemical apparatus, and many the like things. Every man may have occasion to consult books which he does not care to possess, such as cyclopaedias, dictionaries, tables, charts, maps, and public documents: pictures also of birds, beasts, fishes, shells, trees, flowers, whose names he desires to know.

There is a refining influence from the arts of Design on a prepared mind, which is as positive as that of music, and not to be supplied from any other source. But pictures, engravings, statues, and casts, beside their first cost, entail expenses, as of galleries and keepers for the exhibition; and the use which any man can make of them is rare, and their value, too, is much enhanced by the numbers of men who can share their enjoyment. In the Greek cities, it was reckoned profane, that any person should pretend a property in a work of art, which belonged to all who could behold it. I think sometimes,—could I only have music on my own terms;—could I live in a great city, and know where I could go whenever I wished the ablution and inundation of musical waves,—that were a bath and a medicine.

If properties of this kind were owned by states, towns, and lyceums, they would draw the bonds of neighborhood closer. A town would exist to an intellectual purpose. In Europe, where the feudal forms secure the permanence of wealth in certain families, those families buy and preserve these things, and lay them open to the public. But in America, where democratic institutions divide every estate into small portions, after a few years, the public should step into the place of these proprietors, and provide this culture and inspiration for the citizen.

Man was born to be rich, or, inevitably grows rich by the use of his faculties; by the union of thought with nature. Property is an intellectual production. The game requires coolness, right reasoning, promptness, and patience in the players. Cultivated labor drives out brute labor. An infinite number of shrewd men, in infinite years, have arrived at certain best and shortest ways of doing, and this accumulated skill in arts, cultures, harvestings, curings, manufactures, navigations, exchanges, constitutes the worth of our world to-day.

Commerce is a game of skill, which every man cannot play, which few men can play well. The right merchant is one who has the just average of faculties we call common sense; a man of a strong affinity for facts, who makes up his decision on what he has seen. He is thoroughly persuaded of the truths of arithmetic. There is always a reason, in the man, for his good or bad fortune, and so, in making money. Men talk as if there were some magic about this, and believe in magic, in all parts of life. He knows, that all goes on the old road, pound for pound, cent for cent,—for every effect a perfect cause,—and that good luck is another name for tenacity of purpose. He insures himself in every transaction, and likes small and sure gains. Probity and closeness to the facts are the basis, but the masters of the art add a certain long arithmetic. The problem is, to combine many and remote operations, with the accuracy and adherence to the facts, which is easy in near and small transactions; so to arrive at gigantic results, without any compromise of safety. Napoleon was fond of telling the story of the Marseilles banker, who said to his visitor, surprised at the contrast between the splendor of the banker's chateau and hospitality, and the meanness of the counting-room in which he had seen him,—"Young man, you are too young to understand how masses are formed,—the true and only power,—whether composed of money, water, or men, it is all alike,—a mass is an immense centre of motion, but it must be begun, it must be kept up:"—and he might have added, that the way in which it must be begun and kept up, is, by obedience to the law of particles.

Success consists in close appliance to the laws of the world, and, since those laws are intellectual and moral, an intellectual and moral obedience. Political Economy is as good a book wherein to read the life of man, and the ascendency of laws over all private and hostile influences, as any Bible which has come down to us.

Money is representative, and follows the nature and fortunes of the owner. The coin is a delicate meter of civil, social, and moral changes. The farmer is covetous of his dollar, and with reason. It is no waif to him. He knows how many strokes of labor it represents. His bones ache with the day's work that earned it. He knows how much land it represents;—how much rain, frost, and sunshine. He knows that, in the dollar, he gives you so much discretion and patience so much hoeing, and threshing. Try to lift his dollar; you must lift all that weight. In the city, where money follows the skit of a pen, or a lucky rise in exchange, it comes to be looked on as light. I wish the farmer held it dearer, and would spend it only for real bread; force for force.

The farmer's dollar is heavy, and the clerk's is light and nimble; leaps out of his pocket; jumps on to cards and faro-tables: but still more curious is its susceptibility to metaphysical changes. It is the finest barometer of social storms, and announces revolutions.

The value of a dollar is social, as it is created by society. Every man who removes into this city, with any purchasable talent or skill in him, gives to every man's labor in the city, a new worth. If a talent is anywhere born into the world, the community of nations is enriched; and, much more, with a new degree of probity. The expense of crime, one of the principal charges of every nation, is so far stopped. In Europe, crime is observed to increase or abate with the price of bread.

Wealth brings with it its own checks and balances. The basis of political economy is non-interference. The only safe rule is found in the self-adjusting meter of demand and supply. Do not legislate. Meddle, and you snap the sinews with your sumptuary laws. Give no bounties: make equal laws: secure life and property, and you need not give alms. Open the doors of opportunity to talent and virtue, and they will do themselves justice, and property will not be in bad hands. In a free and just commonwealth, property rushes from the idle and imbecile, to the industrious, brave, and persevering.

Our nature and genius force us to respect ends, whilst we use means. We must use the means, and yet, in our most accurate using, somehow screen and cloak them, as we can only give them any beauty, by a reflection of the glory of the end. That is the good head, which serves the end, and commands the means. The rabble are corrupted by their means: the means are too strong for them, and they desert their end.

1. The first of these measures is that each man's expense must proceed from his character. As long as your genius

buys, the investment is safe, though you spend like a monarch. Nature arms each man with some faculty which enables him to do easily some feat impossible to any other, and thus makes him necessary to society. This native determination guides his labor and his spending. He wants an equipment of means and tools proper to his talent. Do your work, respecting the excellence of the work, and not its acceptableness. Nothing is beneath you, if it is in the direction of your life: nothing is great or desirable, if it is off from that. I think we are entitled here to draw a straight line, and say, that society can never prosper, but must always be bankrupt, until every man does that which he was created to do.

Spend for your expense, and retrench the expense which is not yours. Allston, the painter, was wont to say, that he built a plain house, and filled it with plain furniture, because he would hold out no bribe to any to visit him, who had not similar tastes to his own. We are sympathetic, and, like children, want everything we see. But it is a large stride to independence,—when a man, in the discovery of his proper talent, has sunk the necessity for false expenses.

2. Spend after your genius, and by system. Nature goes by rule, not by sallies and saltations. There must be system in the economies. Saving and unexpensiveness will not keep the most pathetic family from ruin, nor will bigger incomes make free spending safe. The secret of success lies never

in the amount of money, but in the relation of income to outgo; as if, after expense has been fixed at a certain point, then new and steady rills of income, though never so small, being added, wealth begins.

3. The rule is not to dictate, nor to insist on carrying out each of your schemes by ignorant wilfulness, but to learn practically the secret spoken from all nature, that things themselves refuse to be mismanaged, and will show to the watchful their own law. Nobody need stir hand or foot. The custom of the country will do it all. I know not how to build or to plant; neither how to buy wood, nor what to do with the house-lot, the field, or the wood-lot, when bought. Never fear: it is all settled how it shall be, long beforehand, in the custom of the country, whether to sand, or whether to clay it, when to plough, and how to dress, whether to grass, or to corn; and you cannot help or hinder it. Nature has her own best mode of doing each thing, and she has somewhere told it plainly, if we will keep our eyes and ears open.

4. Another point of economy is to look for seed of the same kind as you sow: and not to hope to buy one kind with another kind. Friendship buys friendship; justice, justice; military merit, military success. Good husbandry finds wife, children, and household. The good merchant large gains, ships, stocks, and money. The good poet fame, and literary credit; but not either, the other. Yet there is com-

monly a confusion of expectations on these points. Hotspur lives for the moment; praises himself for it; and despises Furlong, that he does not. Hotspur, of course, is poor; and Furlong a good provider. The odd circumstance is, that Hotspur thinks it a superiority in himself, this improvidence, which ought to be rewarded with Furlong's lands.

5. Now these things are so in Nature. All things ascend, and the royal rule of economy is, that it should ascend also, or, whatever we do must always have a higher aim. Thus it is a maxim, that money is another kind of blood. So there is no maxim of the merchant, e.g., "Best use of money is to pay debts;" "Every business by itself;" "Best time is present time;" "The right investment is in tools of your trade;" or the like, which does not admit of an extended sense. The counting-room maxims liberally expounded are laws of the Universe. The merchant's economy is a coarse symbol of the soul's economy. It is, to spend for power, and not for pleasure. It is to invest income; that is to say, to take up particulars into generals; days into integral eras,—literary, emotive, practical, of its life, and still to ascend in its investment. The merchant has but one rule, absorb and invest: he is to be capitalist: the scraps and filings must be gathered back into the crucible; the gas and smoke must be burned, and earnings must not go to increase expense, but to capital again. Well, the man must be capitalist. Will he spend his income, or will he invest? His body and every organ is under the same law. His body is a jar, in which the

liquor of life is stored. Will he spend for pleasure? The way to ruin is short and facile. Will he not spend, but hoard for power? It passes through the sacred fermentations, by that law of Nature whereby everything climbs to higher platforms, and bodily vigor becomes mental and moral vigor. The bread he eats is first strength and animal spirits: it becomes, in higher laboratories, imagery and thought; and in still higher results, courage and endurance. This is the right compound interest; this is capital doubled, quadrupled, centupled; man raised to his highest power.

The true thrift is always to spend on the higher plane; to invest and invest, with keener avarice, that he may spend in spiritual creation, and not in augmenting animal existence. Nor is the man enriched, in repeating the old experiments of animal sensation, nor unless through new powers and ascending pleasures, he knows himself by the actual experience of higher good, to be already on the way to the highest.

About the Author

Born in 1803 in Boston, Massachusetts, RALPH WALDO EMERSON was one of America's preeminent men of letters. The inspiration for the school of philosophy called Transcendentalism, Emerson, in his essays, journals, lectures, and letters, traced out a view of life that located man as an extension and reflection of the Divine, owing his existence and allegiance to none but the highest insights of his own nature. An inspiration on figures ranging from his contemporary Henry David Thoreau to William James, Emerson formulated what can be called the American spiritual vision: non-dogmatic, nonsectarian, and based in the integrity and primacy of the individual spiritual search. In that sense, Emerson is also the founding figure of much of the modern spiritual culture in the West. After many years as a writer, publisher, lecturer, and seeker, he died in 1882 in Concord, Massachusetts, where his house still stands today.

Atom-Smashing
Power of Mind

Atom-Smashing Power of Mind

The Life-Changing Classic on Your Power Within

by Charles Fillmore

THE CONDENSED CLASSICS LIBRARY™

Contents

INTRODUCTION
Charles Fillmore: The Man Who Never Stood Still
by Mitch Horowitz   245

CHAPTER ONE
The Atomic Age   248

CHAPTER TWO
The Restorative Power of Spirit   254

CHAPTER THREE
Spiritual Obedience   258

CHAPTER FOUR
I AM or Superconsciousness   261

CHAPTER FIVE
Day of Judgment   266

CHAPTER SIX
Thou Shalt Decree a Thing 268

CHAPTER SEVEN
Thinking in the Fourth Dimension 270

CHAPTER EIGHT
Is This God's World? 273

CHAPTER NINE
Truth Radiates Light 276

CHAPTER TEN
The Only Mind 280

CHAPTER ELEVEN
The Body 284

CHAPTER TWELVE
Faith Precipitations 288

CHAPTER THIRTEEN
The End of the Age 290

ABOUT THE AUTHOR 294

Introduction

Charles Fillmore: The Man Who Never Stood Still

by Mitch Horowitz

Spiritual experimenters through the ages, from ancient astrologers and alchemists to contemporary chaos magicians and mind-power mystics, have always availed themselves of the latest technologies of their eras. The New Thought pioneer Charles Fillmore, who founded the vibrant and ongoing Unity movement, was a great example of this.

Born in 1854 on an Indian reservation near St. Cloud, Minnesota, Fillmore and his wife and intellectual partner Myrtle, organized their Kansas City-based Unity ministry into one of the nation's first mass-media ministries. As early as 1907, the Fillmores staffed phone banks with round-the-clock volunteers ready to assist callers with distance prayers. The Unity ministry made early use of radio, targeted mailings, correspondence courses, pamphlets, and well-produced magazines aimed at the large demographic range of Unity's congregants. This included the children's monthly *Wee Wisdom*, which launched the literary career of bestselling novelist Sidney Sheldon when it published the ten-year-old's first poem in 1927.

Up to the eve of his death in 1948, Charles Fillmore remained well versed in the science and technology of the newly dawned atomic era. Fillmore sought to unite the insights of science and practical mysticism in the collection of writings that make up *Atom-Smashing Power of the Mind*, which appeared the year after his death.

This 1949 book is one of Fillmore's finest literary efforts. It serves as a powerful and stirring summation of his theology of mind-power metaphysics. At the same time, Fillmore relates the higher abilities of thought to the revolutions in atomic energy that entered public awareness in the years immediately preceding his death. Of this, Fillmore makes a creditable effort, foreseeing future developments in wireless, microwave, and cellular technology. When I consider my failings to stay fully versed in the digital technology of our own era, I am all the more admiring of a frontier boy who grew up not only to establish a major religious denomination but who never stopped learning about the radically changing world around him. Within those changes, Fillmore discovered confirmation of his own universal ideals.

This condensation of *Atom-Smashing Power of Mind* captures the verve, spirit, and soaring language of his original, while retaining his key points and practical insights.

I consider Fillmore's book one of the finest mid-century statements of New Thought philosophy. It is the kind of work that should inspire those of us today who believe that all knowledge—scientific, technological, psychological, medical, and spiritual—ultimately converge. Of this, Charles Fillmore was absolutely certain.

Chapter One

The Atomic Age

The majority of people have crude or distorted ideas about the character and the location of Spirit. They think that Spirit plays no part in mundane affairs and can be known by a person only after his death.

But Jesus said, "God is Spirit;" He also said, "The kingdom of God is within you." Science tells us that there is a universal life that animates and sustains all the forms and shapes of the universe. Science has broken into the atom and revealed it to be charged with tremendous energy that may be released and be made to give the inhabitants of the earth powers beyond expression when its law of expression is discovered.

Jesus evidently knew about this hidden energy in matter and used His knowledge to perform so-called miracles.

Our modern scientists say that a single drop of water contains enough latent energy to blow up a ten-story building. This energy, existence of which has been discovered by modern scientists, is the same kind of spiritual energy that was known to Elijah, Elisha, and Jesus, and used by them to perform miracles.

By the power of his thought Elijah penetrated the atoms and precipitated an abundance of rain. By the same law he increased the widow's oil and meal. This was not a miracle—that is, it was not a divine intervention supplanting natural law—but the exploitation of a law not ordinarily understood. Jesus used the same dynamic power of thought to break the bonds of the atoms composing the few loaves and fishes of a little lad's lunch—and five thousand people were fed.

Science is discovering the miracle-working dynamics of religion, but science has not yet comprehended the dynamic directive power of man's thought. All so-called miracle workers claim that they do not of themselves produce the marvelous results; that they are only the instruments of a superior entity. It is written in I Kings, "The jar of meal wasted not, neither did the cruse of oil fail, according to the word of Jehovah, which he spake by Elijah." Jesus called Jehovah Father. He said, "The works that I do in my Father's name, these bear witness of me."

Jesus did not claim to have the exclusive supernatural power that is usually credited to Him. He had explored the ether energy, which He called the "kingdom of the heavens;" His understanding was beyond that of the average man, but He knew that other men could do what He did if they would only try. He encouraged His followers to take Him as a center of faith and use the power of thought and word. "He that believeth on me, the works that I do shall he do also; and greater works than these shall he do."

Have faith in the power of your mind to penetrate and release the energy that is pent up in the atoms of your body, and you will be astounded at the response. Paralyzed functions anywhere in the body can be restored to action by one's speaking to the spiritual intelligence and life within them. Jesus raised His dead bodies in this way, and Paul says that we can raise our body in the same manner if we have the same spiritual contact.

What have thought concentration and discovery of the dynamic character of the atom to do with prayer? They have everything to do with prayer, because prayer is the opening of communication between the mind of man and the mind of God. Prayer is the exercise of faith in the presence and power of the unseen God. Supplication, faith, meditation, silence, concentration, are mental attitudes that enter into and form part of prayer. When one understands the spiritual character of God and adjusts himself mentally to the omnipresent God-Mind, he has begun to pray rightly.

Audible prayers are often answered but the most potent are silently uttered in the secret recesses of the soul. Jesus warned against wordy prayers—prayer uttered to be heard of men. He told His disciples not to be like those who pray on the housetop. "When thou prayest, enter into thine inner chamber, and having shut thy door, pray to thy Father who is in secret, and thy Father who seeth in secret shall recompense thee."

The times are ripe for great changes in our estimate of the abiding place and the character of God. The six-day creation of the universe (including man) described in Genesis is a symbolic story of the work of the higher realms of mind under divine law. It is the privilege of everyone to use his mind abilities in the superrealms, and thereby carry out the prayer formula of Jesus: "Seek ye first his kingdom, and his righteousness; and all these things shall be added unto you."

Of all the comments on or discussions of the indescribable power of the invisible force released by the atomic bomb none that we have seen mentions its spiritual or mental character. All commentators have written about it as a force external to man to be controlled by mechanical means, with no hint that it is the primal life that animates and interrelates man's mind and body.

The next great achievement of science will be the understanding of the mental and spiritual abilities latent in man through which to develop and release these tremendous electrons, protons, and neutrons secreted in the trillions of cells in the physical organism.

Here is involved the secret, as Paul says, "hid for ages and generations . . . which is Christ [superman] in you, the hope of glory." It is through release of these hidden life forces in his organism that man is to achieve immortal life, and in no other way. When we finally understand the facts of life and rid our minds of the delusion that we shall find immortal life after we die, then we shall seek more diligently to awaken the spiritual man within us and strengthen and build up the spiritual domain of our being until, like Jesus, we shall be able to control the atomic energy in our bodies and perform so-called miracles.

The fact is that all life is based upon the interaction between the various electrical units of the universe. Science tells us about these activities in terms of matter and no one understands them, because they are spiritual entities and their realities can only be understood and used wisely by the spiritually developed man. Electricians do not know what electricity is, although they use it constantly. The Christian uses faith and gets marvelous results, the electrician uses electricity and also gets marvelous results, and neither of them knows the real nature of the agent he uses so freely.

The man who called electricity faith doubtless thought that he was making a striking comparison when in fact he was telling a truth, that faith is of the mind and it is the match that starts the fire in the electrons and protons of innate Spirit forces. Faith has its degrees of voltage; the faith of the child and the faith of the most powerful spiritual adept are far apart in their intensity and results. When the trillions of cells in one's body are roused to expectancy by spiritual faith, a positive spiritual contact results and marvelous transformations take place.

Sir James Jeans, the eminent British scientist, gives a prophecy of this in one of his books. He says in substance that it may be that the gods determining our fate are our own minds working on our brain cells and through them on the world about us.

This will eventually be found to be true, and the discovery of the law of release of the electronic vitality wrapped up in matter will be the greatest revelation of all time.

When we awake to the fact that every breath we draw is releasing this all-potent electronic energy and it is shaping our lives for good or ill, according to our faith, then we shall begin to search for the law that will guide us aright in the use of power.

Chapter Two

The Restorative Power of the Spirit

Not only our Bible but the scriptures of all the nations of the world testify to the existence of an invisible force moving men and nature in their various activities. Not all agree as to the character of this omnipresent force, universal Spirit, but it serves the purpose of being their god under whatever name it may appear. Different nations ostensibly believe in the same scriptures, but they have various concepts of the universal Spirit; some conceive it to be nature and others God. Robert Browning says, "What I call God . . . fools call Nature."

Our Bible plainly teaches that God implanted in man His perfect image and likeness, with executive ability to carry out all the creative plans of the Great Architect. When man arrives at a certain point in spiritual understanding it is his office to cooperate with the God principle in creation.

As the animating life of all things God is a unit, but as the mind that drives this life He is diverse. Every man is king in his own mental domain, and his subjects are his thoughts.

People in this atomic-age civilization ask why God does not reveal Himself now as He did in Bible days. The fact is that God is talking to people everywhere, but they do not understand the message and brush it aside as an idle dream. We need to divest ourselves of the thought that Daniel and Joseph, in fact all the unusually wise men of the Bible, were especially inspired by God, that they were divinely appointed by the Lord to do His work. Everything points to their spiritual insight as the result of work on their part to that end.

The body is the instrument of the mind, and the mind looks to the Spirit for its inspiration. Not only the Scriptures that we look to for authority in our daily living but also the experience of ourselves and our neighbors proves that those who cultivate communion with the Father within become conscious of a guiding light, call it what you will.

Those who scoff at this and say that it is all the work of the imagination are deluding themselves and ignoring a source of instruction and progress that they need above all things. If this sense world were the only world we shall ever know, the attainment of its ambitions might be sufficient for a man of meager outlook and small capacity, but the majority of us see ourselves and the world about us in a process of transformation that will culminate in conditions here on the earth far superior to those we have imagined for heaven.

Jesus was very advanced, and His radiant body was developed in larger degree than that of anyone in our race, but we all have this body, and its development is in proportion to our spiritual culture. In Jesus this body of light glowed "as he was praying." Jesus' body did not go down to corruption, but He, by the intensity of His spiritual devotion, restored every cell to its innate state of atomic light and power. When John was in the state of spiritual devotion Jesus appeared to him, "and his eyes were as a flame of fire; and his feet like unto burnished brass." Jesus lives today in that body of glorified electricity in a kingdom that interpenetrates the earth and its environment. He called it the kingdom of the heavens.

We do not have to look to the many experiences recorded in the Bible of the spiritually illumined to prove the existence of the spiritual supersubstance. People everywhere are discovering it, as they always have in every age and clime.

The metaphysical literature of our day is very rich with the experiences of those who have found through various channels the existence of the radiant body. This prompts me to tell of my development of the radiant body, during half a century's experience. It began when I was mentally affirming statements of Truth. Just between my eyes, but above, I felt a "thrill" that lasted a few moments, then passed away. I found I could repeat this experience with affirmations. As time went on I could set up this "thrill" at other points in my body and finally it became a continuous current throughout my nervous system. I called it "the Spirit" and found that it was connected with a universal life force whose source was the Christ. As taught in the Bible, we have through wrong thinking and living lost contact with the parent life. Jesus Christ incarnated in the flesh and thereby introduced us by His Word into the original Father life. He said, "If a man keep my word, he shall never taste of death." I have believed that and affirmed His words until they have become organized in my body. Sometimes when I make this claim of Christ life in the body I am asked if I expect to live always in this flesh. My answer is that I realize that the flesh is being broken down every day and its cells transformed into energy and life, and a new body is being formed of a very superior quality. That new body in Christ will be my future habitation.

I have found that the kingdom of God is within man and that we are wasting our time and defeating the work of the Spirit if we look for it anywhere else.

Chapter Three
Spiritual Obedience

Zeal is the great universal force that impels man to spring forward in a field of endeavor and accomplish the seemingly miraculous. It is the inward fire that urges man onward, regardless of the intellectual mind of caution and conversation.

Zeal should be tempered with wisdom. It is possible to be so zealously active on the intellectual plane that one's vitality is consumed and there is nothing left for spiritual growth. "Take time to be holy." Never neglect your soul. To grow spiritually you should exercise your zeal in spiritual ways.

Above all other Bible writers Paul emphasizes the importance of the mind in the transformation of character and body. In this respect he struck a note in religion that had been mute up to this time; that is, that spirit and mind are akin and that man is related to God through his thought. Paul sounds again and again in various forms this silent but very essential chord in the unity of God and man and man and his body.

When the scientific world investigates the so-called miracles of religion and discovers that they are being duplicated continually, the power of mind over matter will be heralded as of great importance to both religion and science.

Prayer gives spiritual poise to the ego, and it brings forth eternal life when spiritually linked with the Christ. "If a man keep my word, he shall never see death."

To one who gains even a meager quickening of the Spirit, Christianity ceases to be a theory; it becomes a demonstrable science of the mind.

We must not anticipate better social and economic conditions until we have better men and women to institute and sustain those conditions.

Jesus said that He was the bread and substance that came down from heaven. When will our civilization begin to realize and appropriate this mighty ocean of substance and life?

A finer civilization than now exists has been conceived by many from Plato in his "Republic" to Edward Bellamy in "Looking Backward." But a new and higher civilization will be developed only through the efforts of higher and finer types of men and women. Philosophers and seers have looked forward to a time when this earth would produce superior men and women, but save Jesus none has had the spiritual insight to declare, "Verily I say unto you, This generation shall not pass away, until all these things be accomplished."

"Behold, the man!" Jesus Christ is the type of a new race now forming in the earth. Those who incorporate into consciousness the Christ principles are its members.

The dominion that God gave to man in the beginning, as recorded in Genesis, is a dominion over spiritual ideas, which are represented in the allegory by material symbols.

Hence to exercise his dominion man must understand the metaphysical side of everything in existence.

Divine Mind is the one and only reality. When we incorporate the ideas that form Divine Mind into our mind and persevere in those ideas, a mighty strength wells up within us. Then we have a foundation for the spiritual body, the body not made with hands, eternal in the heavens. When the spiritual body is established in consciousness, its strength and power is transmitted to the visible body and to all the things that we touch in the world about us.

In the economy of the future man will not be a slave to money. Humanity's daily needs will be met in ways not now thought practical.

In the new economy we shall serve for the joy of serving, and prosperity will flow to us and through us in rippling streams of plenty. The supply and support that love and zeal set in motion are not yet largely used by man, but those who have tested this method are loud in their praise of its efficiency.

Chapter Four

I AM or Superconciousness

Superconciousness is the goal toward which humanity is working. Regardless of appearances there is an upward trend continually active throughout all creation. The superconsciousness is the realm of divine ideas. Its character is impersonal. It therefore has no personal ambitions; knows no condemnation; but is always pure, innocent, loving, and obedient to the call of God.

The superconsciousness has been perceived by the spiritually wise in every age, but they have not known how to externalize it and make it an abiding state of consciousness. Jesus accomplished this, and His method is worthy of our adoption, because as far as we know, it is the only method that has been successful. It is set forth in the New Testament, and whoever adopts the life of purity and love and power there exemplified in the experiences of Jesus of Nazareth will in due course attain the place that He attained.

Jesus acknowledged Himself to be the Son of God. Living in the superconsciousness calls for nothing less on our part than a definite recognition of ourselves as sons of God right here and now, regardless of appearances to the contrary. We know that we are sons of God; then why not acknowledge it and proceed to take possession of our God heirdom? That is what Jesus did in the face of the most adverse conditions. Conditions today are not so inertly material as they were in Jesus' time. People now know more about themselves and their relation to God. They are familiar with thought processes and how an idea held in mind will manifest itself in the body and in affairs; hence they take up this problem of spiritual realization under vastly more favorable conditions. An idea must work out just as surely as a mathematical problem, because it is under immutable law. The factors are all in our possession, and the method was demonstrated in one striking instance and is before us. By following the method of Jesus and doing day-by-day work that comes to us, we shall surely put on Christ as fully and completely as did Jesus of Nazareth.

The method by which Jesus evolved from sense consciousness to God consciousness was, first, the recognition of the spiritual selfhood and a constant affirmation of its supremacy and power. Jesus loved to make the highest statements: "I and the Father are one." "All authority hath been given unto me in heaven and on earth." He made these statements, so we know that at the time He was fully aware of their reality. Secondly, by the power of His word He penetrated deeper into omnipresence and tapped the deepest resources of His mind, whereby He released the light, life, and substance of Spirit, which enabled Him to get the realization that wholly united His consciousness with the Father Mind.

In the light of modern science the miracles of the Bible can be rationally explained as Mind acting in an omnipresent spiritual field, which is open to all men who develop spiritually. "Ye who have followed me, in the regeneration when the Son of man shall sit on the throne of his glory, ye also shall sit upon twelve thrones, judging the twelve tribes of Israel."

"He that overcometh, I will give to him to sit down with me in my throne."

Overcoming is a change of mind from error to Truth. The way of overcoming is first to place one's self by faith in the realization of Sonship, and second, to demonstrate it in every thought and act.

The Word is man's I AM. The Holy Spirit is the "outpouring" or activity of the living Word. The work of the Holy Spirit is the executive power of Father (mind) and Son (idea), carrying out the creative plan. It is through the help of the Holy Spirit that man overcomes. The Holy Spirit reveals, helps, and directs in this overcoming. "The Spirit searcheth all things, yea, the deep things of God." It finally leads man into the light.

Science rightly understood is of inestimable value to religion, and Christianity in order to become the world power that its founder envisioned, must stress the unfoldment of the spiritual mind in man in order that he may do the mighty works promised by Jesus.

When Jesus went up into the mount to pray He was transfigured before His apostles

Peter, James, and John. True prayer brings about an exalted radiation of energy, and when it is accompanied by faith, judgment, and love, the word of Truth bursts forth in a stream of light that, when held in mind, illumines, uplifts, and glorifies.

Jesus recognized Mind in everything and called it "Father." He knew that there is a faith center in each atom of so-called matter and that faith in man can move upon the faith center in so-called matter and can remove mountains.

Jesus taught that the realities of God are capable of expression here in this world and that man within himself has God capacity and power. Jesus was crucified because He claimed to be the Son of God. Yet the Scriptures, which the Pharisees worshiped, had this bold proclamation, which Jesus quoted to them from Psalms 82:

"I said, Ye are gods,
And all of you sons of the Most High."

The reports by His followers of what He taught clearly point to two subjects that He loved to discourse upon. The first was the Son of God: He was the Son of God. Secondly: We might all become as He was and demonstrate our dominion by following Him in the regeneration.

In order to follow Jesus in the regeneration we must become better acquainted with the various phases of mind and how they function in and through the body.

In spiritual understanding we know that all the forces in the body are directed by thought and that they work in a constructive or a destructive way, according to the character of the thought. Medicine, massage, and all the material means accomplish but incomplete, unsatisfactory, temporary results, because they work only from the outside and do not touch the inner springs that control the forces. The springs can only be touched by thought. There must be a unity between the mind of man and Divine Mind so that ideas and thoughts that work constructively unto eternal life may be quickened in the mind and organism of man.

We are told in John that the world could not contain the books that would be written if all the things that Jesus did were put into writing. But enough is given in the story of His life and in the writings of the apostles concerning Him to bear witness to that which is daily being revealed in this day of fulfillment. Those who are consecrated to Truth and fully resolved to follow Jesus all the way are spiritualizing the whole man, including the body, which is being redeemed from corruption. Those who are living as Jesus lived are becoming like Him. "God is not the God of the dead, but of the living." Resurrection takes place in people who are alive.

Chapter Five

The Day of Judgment

It is said we are to be judged after death according to deeds done in the body, which are kept on record like books that are balanced; and if the balance is found to be in our favor we go up, and if against us we go down. But if we are spiritual now—divine—this spiritual part has dominion, and we begin to exercise this dominion. The moment we catch sight of this we begin to judge. We begin to put the thoughts that are good on the right and the others on the left. All our ideas of the attributes of our divine self we put on the right hand of power, while the thoughts of disease, death, limitation and lack we put on the left—denied, cut off.

This is not to occur after death. It is to begin right now!

Now is the time to plant the seed thought of the conditions we desire by saying, "Come my good thoughts, let us inherit our kingdom."

We do not fear anything, for we have separated our sheep from our goats; we have set our true thoughts on the right and have denied our error thoughts any power whatever.

Come into the kingdom of mind. Here everything that is in Principle is yours.

Everything, all good, is to be gathered up, and everything is good at its center. The essence of your body is good and of true substance. When you sift your consciousness of all but the real and true, the body becomes full of light.

The diamond owes its brilliance to the perfect arrangement of the innumerable little prisms within it, each of which refracts the light of the other. Man's body is made up of centers of consciousness—of light—and if arranged so they radiate the light within you, you will shine like the diamond. All things are in the consciousness and you have to learn to separate the erroneous from the true, darkness from light. The I AM must separate the sheep from the goats. This sifting begins right now and goes on until the perfect child of God is manifest and you are fully rounded out in all your Godlike attributes

Chapter Six
Thou Shalt Decree a Thing

To decree with assurance is to establish and fix an ideal in substance. The force behind the decree is invisible, like a promise to be fulfilled at a future time; but it binds with its invisible chains the one who makes it. We have only a slight conception of the strength of the intangible. We compare and measure strength by some strong element in nature. We say "strong as steel." But a very little thought will convince us that mental affirmations are far stronger than the strongest visible thing in the world. The reason for this is that visible things lack livingness. They are not linked with energy and intelligence as are words. Words charged with power and intelligence increase with use, while material things decrease.

It is not necessary to call the attention of metaphysicians to the fact that all visible things had their origin in the invisible. The visible is what remains of an idea that has gradually lost its energy. Scientists say that this so-called solid earth under our feet was once radiant substance. Nothing is really "solid" but the atomic energy latent in everything. They tell us that it takes some six billion years for uranium to disintegrate and become lead, and this rate of disintegration has helped scientists determine the age of the earth as about two billion years.

Since nothing is lost in the many transformations that occur in nature, what becomes of the energy that is being released in the disintegration that is going on in our earth? The answer is that a new earth is being formed in which matter will be replaced by atomic energy. This process of refining matter into radiant substance is taking place not only in the natural world but in our bodies also. In fact the speed with which the transformation takes place depends on the character of the thoughts that we project into our brains and through them into our bodies and the world about us. This is why we should spiritualize our thoughts and refine the food we eat to correspond.

At the present writing there is a housing shortage everywhere and the lack of materials and competent labor indicate that several years will elapse before the need is met. This is counted a calamity; but is it? The inventive genius of man is planning houses of glass and other materials that will be much less expensive—more durable and in every respect superior to the present homes. When man gets his ingenious mind into action he always meets every emergency with something better. Every adverse situation can be used as a spur to urge one to greater exertion and the ultimate attainment of some ideal that has lain dormant in the subconsciousness.

CHAPTER SEVEN

Thinking in the Fourth Dimension

Scientists tell us that the discoveries that their efforts are revealing convince them that they are just on the verge of stupendous truths. Christianity spiritually interpreted shows that Jesus understood the deeper things of God's universe. He understood exactly what the conditions were on the invisible side of life, which is termed in His teaching the "kingdom of God" or the "kingdom of the heavens." We are trying to connect His teaching with modern science in order to show the parallel; but as He said in Mark 4:23, "if any man hath ears to hear, let him hear." This means that we must develop a capacity for understanding in terms of the atomic structure of the universe.

Unless we have this spiritual capacity we do not understand. We think we have ears, but they are attuned to materiality. They do not get the radiations from the supermind, the Christ Mind. Physiology working with psychology is demonstrating that hearing and seeing can be developed in every cell in the body, independent of ears and eyes. We hear and see with our minds working through our bodies. This being true, the capacity to hear may extend beyond the physical ear into the spiritual ethers, and we should be able to hear the voice of God.

This extension of hearing is what Jesus taught. "If any man hath ears to hear, let him hear."

Then we are told that we must "take heed" what we hear. Many of us have found that as we develop this inner, spiritual hearing, we hear voices sometimes that do not tell the truth. These deceptive voices can be hushed by affirming the presence and power of the Lord Jesus Christ.

As you unfold your spiritual nature, you will find that it has the same capacity for receiving vibrations of sound as your outer, physical ear has. You do not give attention to all that you hear in the external; you discriminate as you listen. So in the development of this inner, spiritual ear take heed what you hear: discriminate.

Jesus said, "For he that hath, to him shall be given: and he that hath not, from him shall be taken away even that which he hath." How can what a man has not be taken away? We believe in our mortal consciousness that we have attained a great deal, but if we have not this inner, spiritual consciousness of reality our possessions are impermanent. Then we must be careful what we accumulate in our consciousness, because "he that hath, to him shall be given." The more spiritual Truth you pile up in your mind, the more you have of reality, and the larger is your capacity for the unlimited; but if you have nothing of a spiritual character, what little you have of intellectual attainment will eventually be taken away from you.

The mysteries of the supermind have always been considered the property of certain schools of occultists and mystics who were cautious about giving their truths to the masses for fear that in their ignorance these might misuse them. But now the doors are thrown wide open, and whosoever will may enter in.

Our attention in this day is being largely called to the revolution that is taking place in the economic world, but a revolution of even greater worth is taking place in the mental and spiritual worlds. A large and growing school of metaphysicians has made its advent in this generation, and it is radically changing the public mind toward religion. In other words, we are developing spiritual understanding, and this means that religion and its sources in tradition and in man are being inquired into and its principles applied in the development of a new cosmic mind for the whole human family.

Chapter Eight

Is This God's World?

"Why doesn't God do something about it?" This oft-repeated query, uttered by the skeptical and unbelieving, is heard day in and day out. Imitating the skeptics, Christian believers everywhere are looking to God for all kinds of reforms in every department of manifest life and also are charging Him with death and destruction the world over.

One who thinks logically and according to sound reason wonders at the contradictions set up by these various queries and desires.

Is God responsible for all that occurs on this earth, and if not all, how much of it?

The Bible states that God created the earth and all its creatures, and last of all man, to whom He gave dominion over everything. Observation and experience prove that man is gaining dominion over nature wherever he applies himself to that end. But so much remains to be gained, and he is so small physically that man counts himself a pygmy instead of the mental giant that he is.

All the real mastery that man attains in the world has its roots in his mind, and when he opens up the mental realm in his being there are no unattainables. If the conquests of the air achieved in the last quarter century had been prophesied, the prophets would have been pronounced crazy. The fact is that no one thinking in the old mind realm can have any conception of the transformation of sound waves into electromagnetic waves and back again into words and messages of intelligence. Edison admitted that his discovery of the phonograph was an accident and that he never fully understood how mechanical vibrations could be recorded and be reproduced in all forms of intelligent communication.

Now that man has broken away from his limited visualizations and mentally grasped the unhampered ideas of the supermind, he is growing grandly bold and his technical pioneers are telling him that the achievements of yesterday are as nothing compared to those of tomorrow. For example, an article by Harland Manchester condensed in the *Reader's Digest* from *Scientific American* tells of the "microwaves" that are slated for a more spectacular career in the realm of the unbelievable than anything that has preceded them. This article describes in detail some of the marvels that will evolve out of the utilization of microwaves, among which may be mentioned "private phone calls by the hundreds of thousands sent simultaneously over the same wave band without wires, poles or cables. Towns where each citizen has his own radio frequency, over which he can get voice, music, and television, and call any phone in the country by dialing. Complete abolition of static and interference from electrical devices and from other stations. A hundred times as much 'space on the air' as we now have in the commercial radio band. A high-definition and color television network to cover the country. And, perhaps most important of all, a nationwide radar network, geared to television, to regulate all air traffic and furnish instantaneous visual weather reports to airfields throughout the land."

Add to this the marvels promised by the appliers of atomic energy and you have an array of miracles unequaled in all the bibles of all the nations of the world.

It is admitted by those who are most familiar with the dynamic power of these newly discovered forces that we do not yet know how to protect our body cells from the destructiveness of their vibrations. Very thick concrete walls are required to protect those who experiment with atomic forces. One scientist says that the forces released from the bombs that were used on the Japanese cities in 1945 may affect those who were subjected to them and their descendants for a thousand years. Experimentation proves that we have tapped a kingdom that we do not know how to handle safely.

Chapter Nine

Truth Radiates Light

Spiritual light transcends in glory all the laws of matter and intellect. Even Moses could not enter the Tabernacle when it was aglow with this transcendent light.

It is written that the Israelites did not go forward on days when the cloud remained over the Tabernacle, but when the cloud was taken up they went forward. This means that there is no soul progress for man when his body is under the shadow of a "clouded" mind, but when the cloud is removed there is an upward and forward movement of the whole consciousness (all the people).

We are warned of the effect of thoughts that are against or opposed to the commandments of Jehovah. When we murmur and complain we cloud our minds, and Divine Mind cannot reach us or help us. Then we usually loaf until something turns up that causes us to think on happier things, when we go forward again.

Instead of giving up to circumstances and outer events we should remember that we are all very close to a kingdom of mind that would make us always happy and successful if we would cultivate it and make it and its laws a vital part of our life. "The joy of Jehovah is your strength."

You ask, "How can I feel the joy of Jehovah when I am poor, or sick, or unhappy?"

Jesus said, "Come unto me, all ye that labor and are heavy laden, and I will give you rest."

Here is the first step in getting out of the mental cloud that obscures the light of Spirit. Take the promises of Jesus as literally and spiritually true. Right in the midst of the most desperate situation one can proclaim the presence and power of Christ, and that is the first mental move in dissolving the darkness. You cannot think of Jesus without a feeling of freedom and light. Jesus taught freedom from mortality and proclaimed His glory so persistently that He energized our thought atmosphere into light.

The Scriptures state that when Moses came down from Mount Sinai with the Ten Commandments his face shone so brilliantly that the Children of Israel and even Aaron, his own brother, were afraid to come near him until he put a veil over his face. The original Hebrew says his face sent forth beams or horns of light.

The Vulgate says that Moses had "a horned face;" which Michelangelo took literally, in his statue of Moses representing him with a pair of horns projecting from the head. Thus we see the ludicrous effect of reading the Bible according to the letter.

Our men of science have experimented with the brain in action, and they tell us that it is true that we radiate beams when we think. The force of these beams has been measured.

Here we have further confirmation of the many statements in the Bible that have been taken as ridiculous and unbelievable or as miracles.

Persons who spend much time in prayer and meditate a great deal on spiritual things develop the same type of face that Moses is said to have had. We say of them that their faces fairly shine when they talk about God and His love. John saw Jesus on the island of Patmos, and he says, "His countenance was as the sun shineth in his strength."

I have witnessed this radiance in the faces of Truth teachers hundreds of times. I well remember one class lesson during which the teacher became so eloquent that beams of light shot forth from her head and tongues of fire flashed through the room, very like those which were witnessed when the followers of Jesus were gathered in Jerusalem.

We now know that fervent words expressed in prayer and song and eloquent proclamations of spiritual Truth release the millions of electrons in our brain cells and through them blend like chords of mental music with the Mind universal.

This tendency on our part to analyze and scientifically dissect the many supposed miracles recorded in the Bible is often regarded as sacrilegious, or at least as making commonplaces of some of the very spectacular incidents recorded in Scripture.

In every age preceding this the priesthood has labored under the delusion that the common people could not understand the real meaning of life and that they should therefore be kept in ignorance of its inner sources; also that the masses could not be trusted with sacred truths, that imparting such truths to them was like casting pearls before swine.

But now science is delving into hidden things, and it is found that they all arise in and are sustained by universal principles that are open to all men who seek to know and apply them.

Anyone who will search for the science in religion and the religion in science will find that they harmonize and prove each other. The point of unity is the Spirit-mind common to both. So long as religion assumes that the Spirit that creates and sustains man and the universe can be cajoled and by prayer or some other appeal can be induced to change its laws, it cannot hope to be recognized by those who know that unchangeable law rules everywhere and in everything.

Again, so long as science ignores the principle of intelligence in the evolutionary and directive forces of man and the universe, just so long will it fail to understand religion and the power of thought in the changes that are constantly taking place in the world, visible and invisible.

Chapter Ten

The Only Mind

I say, "An idea comes to me." Where did it come from? It must have had a source of like character with its own. Ideas are not visible to the eye, they are not heard by the ear, nor felt, nor tasted, yet we talk about them as having existence. We recognize that they live, move, and have being in the realm that we term mind.

This realm of mind is accepted by everybody as in some way connected with the things that appear, but because it is not describable in terms of length, breadth, and thickness, it is usually passed over as something too vague for consideration.

But those who take up the study of this thing called mind find that it can be analyzed and its laws and modes of operation understood.

To be ignorant of mind and its laws is to be a child playing with fire, or a man manipulating powerful chemicals without knowing their relation to one another. This is universally true; and all who are not learning about mind are in like danger, because all are dealing with the great cause from which spring forth all the conditions that appear in the lives of all men and women. Mind is the one reservoir from which we draw all that we make up into our world, and it is through the laws of mind that we form our lives. Hence nothing is as important as a knowledge of mind, its inherencies, and the mode of their expression.

The belief that mind cannot be understood is fallacious. Man is the expression of mind, dwells in mind, and can know more clearly and definitely about the mind than the things that appear in the phenomenal world.

Mind is the great storehouse of good from which man draws all his supplies. If you manifest life, you are confident that it had a source. If you show forth intelligence you know that somewhere in the economy of Being there is a fount of intelligence. So you may go over the elements that go to make up your being and you will find that they draw their sustenance from an invisible and, to your limited understanding, incomprehensible source.

This source we term Mind, because it is as such that our comprehension is best related to it. Names are arbitrary, and we should not stop to note differences that are merely technical. We want to get at the substance which they represent.

So if we call this invisible source Mind it is because it is of like character with the thing within our consciousness that we call our mind. Mind is manyfold in its manifestations. It produces all that appears. Not that the character of all that appears is to be laid to the volition of Mind; no, but some of its factors enter into everything that appears. This is why it is so important to know about Mind, and how its potentialities are made manifest.

And this is where we have set up a study that makes of every atom in the universe a living center of wisdom as well as life and substance.

We claim that on its plane of comprehension man may ask the atom or the mountain the secret that it holds and it will be revealed to him. This is the communication of mind with Mind; hence we call Mind the universal underlying cause of existence and study it from that basis.

God is Mind, and man made in the image and likeness of God is Mind, because there is but one Mind, and that is the Mind of God. The person in sense consciousness thinks he has a mind of his own and that he creates thought from its own inherent substance. This is a suppositional mind that passes away when the one and only real Mind is revealed. This one and only Mind of God that we study is the only creator. It is that which originates all that is permanent; hence it is the source of all reality. Its creations are of a character hard for the sense man to comprehend, because his consciousness is cast in a mold of space and time. These are changeable and transient, while the creations of the one Mind are substantial and lasting. But it is man's privilege to understand the creations of the one Mind, for it is through them that he makes his world. The creations of the one Mind are ideas. The ideas of God are potential forces waiting to be set in motion through proper formative vehicles. The thinking faculty in man is such a vehicle, and it is through this that the visible universe has existence. Man does not "create" anything if by this term is meant the producing of something from nothing; but he does make the formless up into form; or rather it is through his conscious cooperation that the one Mind forms its universe.

Mind is the storehouse of ideas. Man draws all his ideas from this omnipresent storehouse. The ideas of God, heaven, hell, devils, angels, and all things have their clue in Mind. But their form in the consciousness depends entirely upon the plane from which man draws his mental images. If he gets a "clue" to the character of God and then proceeds to clothe this clue idea with images from without, he makes God a mortal. If he looks within for the clothing of his clue idea he knows God to be the omnipresent Spirit of existence.

So it is of the utmost importance that we know how we have produced this state of existence which we call life; and we should be swift to conform to the only method calculated to bring harmony and success into our life, namely to think in harmony with the understanding derived from communion with the God-Mind.

Chapter Eleven
The Body

You see at once that man is not body, but that the body is the declaration of man, the substantial expression of his mind. We see so many different types of men that we are bound to admit that the body is merely the individual's specific interpretation of himself, whatever it may be. Man is an unknown quantity; we see merely the various ideas of man expressed in terms of body, but not man himself. The identification of man is determined by the individual himself, and he expresses his conception of man in his body.

Some persons have tall bodies; some have short ones. Some have fat bodies; some have slim ones. Some have distorted bodies, some have symmetrical ones. Now, if the body is the man, as claimed by sense consciousness, which of these many bodies is man?

The Bible declares that man is made in the "image" and after the "likeness" of God. Which of the various bodies just enumerated is the image and likeness of God?

Let us repeat that the body of man is the visible record of his thoughts. It is the individual's interpretation of his identity, and each individual shows in his body just what his views of man are. The body is the corporeal record of the mind of its owner, and there is no limit to its infinite differentiation. The individual may become any type of being that he elects to be. Man selects the mental model and the body images it. So the body is the image and likeness of the individual's idea of man. We may embody any conception of life or being that we can conceive. The body is the exact reproduction of the thoughts of its occupant. As a man thinks in his mind so is his body.

You can be an Adam if you choose, or you can be a Christ or any other type of being that you see fit to ideate. The choice lies with you. The body merely executes the mandates of the mind. The mind dictates the model according to which the body shall be manifested. Therefore as man "thinketh within himself [in his vital nature], so is he." Each individual is just what he believes he is.

It is safe to say that nine hundred and ninety-nine persons out of every thousand believe that the resurrection of the body has something specifically to do with the getting of a new body after death; so we find more than ninety-nine per cent of the world's population waiting for death to get something new in the way of a body. This belief is not based on the principles of Truth, for there is no ready-made-body factory in the universe, and thus none will get the body that he expects. Waiting for death in order to get a new body is the folly of ignorance. The thing to do is to improve the bodies that we now have; it can be done, and those who would follow Jesus in the regeneration must do it.

The "resurrection" of the body has nothing whatever to do with death, except that we may resurrect ourselves from every dead condition into which sense ignorance has plunged us. To be resurrected means to get out of the place that you are in and to get into another place. Resurrection is a rising into new vigor, new prosperity; a restoration to some higher state. It is absurd to suppose that it applies only to the resuscitation of a dead body.

It is the privilege of the individual to express any type of body that he sees fit to ideate. Man may become a Christ in mind and in body by incorporating into his every thought the ideas given to the world by Jesus.

Divine mind has placed in the mind of everyone an image of the perfect-man body. The imaging process in the mind may well be illustrated by the picture that is made by light on the photographic plate, which must be "developed" before it becomes visible. Or man's invisible body may be compared to the blueprint of a building that the architect delivers to the builder. Man is a builder of flesh and blood. Jesus was a carpenter. Also He was indeed the master mason. He restored the Lord's body ("the temple of Jehovah") in His mind and heart (in Jerusalem).

The resurrection of the body is not dependent for its demonstration on time, evolution, or any of the man-made means of growth. It is the result of the elevation of the spiritually emancipated mind of the individual.

Step by step, thought added to thought, spiritual emotion added to spiritual emotion—eventually the transformation is complete. It does not come in a day, but every high impulse, every pure thought, every upward desire adds to the exaltation and gradual personification of the divine in man and to the transformation of the human. The "old man" is constantly brought into subjection, and his deeds forever put off, as the "new man" appears arrayed in the vestments of divine consciousness.

How to accomplish the resurrection of the body has been the great stumbling block of man. The resurrection has been a mere hope, and we have endeavored to reconcile a dying body with a living God, but have not succeeded. No amount of Christian submission or stoical philosophy will take away the sting of death. But over him who is risen in Christ "death no more hath dominion."

Chapter Twelve
Faith Precipitations

When asked what electricity is, a scientist replied that he had often thought of it as an adjunct to faith, judging from the way it acts.

This linking of faith and electricity seems at first glance fantastic, but when we observe what takes place when certain substances in solution and an electric current are brought in conjunction, there seems to be a confirmation of the Scripture passage: "Now faith is assurance of things hoped for."

Just as the electric current precipitates certain metals in solution in acid, so faith stirs into action the electrons of man's brain; and acting concurrently with the spiritual ethers, these electrons hasten nature and produce quickly what ordinarily requires months of seedtime and harvest.

Speedy answers to prayer have always been experienced and always will be when the right relations are established between the mind of the one who prays and the spiritual realm, which is like an electrical field. The power to perform what seems to be miracles has been relegated to some God-selected one; but now we are inquiring into the law, since God is no respecter of persons, and we find that the fulfillment of the law rests with man or a group of men, when they quicken by faith the spiritual forces latent within them.

The reason why some prayers are not answered is lack of proper adjustment of the mind of the one who prays to the omnipresent creative spiritual life.

Jesus was the most successful demonstrator of prayer of whom we have any record, and He urged persistence in prayer. If at first you don't succeed, try, try again. Like Lincoln, Jesus loved to tell stories to illustrate His point, and He emphasized the value of persistence in prayer. He told of a woman who demanded justice of a certain judge and importuned him until in sheer desperation he granted her request.

Every Christian healer has had experiences where persistent prayer saved his patient. If he had merely said one prayer, as if giving a prescription for the Lord to fill, he would have fallen far short of demonstrating the law. Elijah prayed persistently until the little cloud appeared or, as we should say, he had a "realization;" then the manifestation followed.

Chapter Thirteen
The End of the Age

In all ages and among all people, there have been legends of prophets and saviors and predictions of their coming.

The fact that all who believe in the principle of divine incarnation have long strained their eyes across the shining sands in an effort to catch sight of the coming of one clothed with the power of heaven, should make us pause and consider the cause of such universality of opinion among peoples widely separated. To dismiss the subject as a religious superstition is not in harmony with unprejudiced reason. To regard these prophecies merely as religious superstitions rules out traditions that are as tenable and as reliable as the facts of history. There is a cause for every effect, and the cause underlying this almost unanimous expectation of a messiah must have some of the omnipresence of a universal law.

In considering a subject like this, which demonstrates itself largely on metaphysical lines, it is necessary to look beyond the material plane to the realm of causes.

The material universe is but the shadow of the spiritual universe. The pulsations of the spiritual forces impinge upon and sway men, nations, and planets, according to laws whose sweep in space and time is so stupendous as to be beyond the ken or comprehension of astronomy. But the fact should not be overlooked that higher astronomy had its votaries in the past. The Magi and the illumined sages of Chaldea and Egypt had astronomical knowledge of universal scope. It was so broad, so gigantic, so far removed from the comprehension of the common mind of their day that it always remained the property of the few. It was communicated in symbols, because of the poverty of language to express its supermundane truths. In the sacred literature of the Hindus are evidences of astronomical erudition covering such vast periods of time that modern philosophers cannot or do not give them credence, and they are relegated to the domain of speculation rather than of science. However the astronomers of the present age have forged along on material lines until now they are beginning to impinge upon the hidden wisdom of the mighty savants of the past.

There is evidence that proves that the ages of the distant past knew a higher astronomy than do we of this age, and that they predicted the future of this planet through cycles and aeons—its nights of mental darkness and the dawn of its spiritual day—with the same accuracy that our astronomers do its present-day planetary revolutions.

Jesus evidently understood the aeons or ages through which earth passes. For example, in Matthew 13:39, our English Bible reads: "The enemy that sowed them is the devil: and the harvest is the end of the world; and the reapers are angels." In the Diaglott version, which gives the original

Greek and a word-for-word translation, this reads: "THAT ENEMY who SOWED them is the ADVERSARY; the HARVEST is the End of the Age; and the REAPERS are Messengers." In this as in many other passages where Jesus used the word "age," it has been translated "world," leading the reader to believe that Jesus taught that this planet was to be destroyed.

So we see that the almost universally accepted teaching of the end of the world is not properly founded on the Bible. The translators wanted to give the wicked a great scare, so they put "the end of the world" into Jesus' mouth in several instances where He plainly said "the end of the age."

The Bible is a textbook of absolute Truth; but its teachings are veiled in symbol and understood only by the illumined.

In accordance with the prophecies of the ancients, our planetary system has just completed a journey of 2,169 years, in which there has been wonderful material progress without its spiritual counterpart. But old conditions have passed away and a new era has dawned. A great change is taking place in the mentality of the race, and this change is evidenced in literature, science, and religion. There is a breaking away from old creeds and old doctrines, and there is a tendency to form centers along lines of scientific spiritual thought. The literature of the first half of the twentieth century is so saturated with occultism as to be an object of censure by conservatives, who denounce it as a "lapse into the superstition of the past." Notwithstanding the protests of the conservatives, on every hand are evidences of spiritual freedom; it crops out in so many ways that an enumeration would cover the whole field of life.

It is evident that Jesus and His predecessors had knowledge of coming events on lines of such absolute accuracy as to place it in the realm of truth ascertained, that is, exact science.

Do you belong to the old, or are you building anew from within and keeping time with the progress of the age? The "harvest" or "consummation of the age" pointed out by Jesus is not far off. This is no theological scare; it is a statement based on a law that is now being tested and proved.

Listen to your inner voice; cultivate the good, the pure, the God within you. Do not let your false beliefs keep you in the darkness of error until you go out like a dying ember. The divine spark is within you. Fan it into flame by right thinking, right living, and right doing, and you will find the "new Jerusalem."

About the Author

One of the pioneering leaders of the New Thought movement, CHARLES FILLMORE (1884–1948), with his wife Myrtle, founded the worldwide Unity ministry. An early visionary in using mass media to spread religious and inspirational messages, Fillmore was widely known for his metaphysical interpretations of the Bible, and for his books including *Prosperity; Christian Healing; Talks on Truth; Atom-Smashing Power of Mind*; and *The Twelve Powers*.

About Mitch Horowitz

MITCH HOROWITZ is the PEN Award-winning author of books including *Occult America* and *The Miracle Club*. A writer-in-residence at the New York Public Library and lecturer-in-residence at the University of Philosophical Research in Los Angeles, Mitch introduces and edits G&D Media's line of Condensed Classics and is the author of the Napoleon Hill Success Course series, including *The Miracle of a Definite Chief Aim*, *The Power of the Master Mind*, and *Secrets of Self-Mastery*. He is on Twitter @MitchHorowitz and on Instagram @MitchHorowitz23.

www.ingramcontent.com/pod-product-compliance
Lightning Source LLC
Chambersburg PA
CBHW071223080526
44587CB00013BA/1472